THE REALITY

OF GOD

LOUIS CASSELS

HERALD PRESS • Scottdale, Pennsylvania

THE REALITY OF GOD

...ns for Herald Press by
...ompany, Inc.

...ugust, 1972

... Number: 71-150879

...ls

Printed in the United States of America

HERALD PRESS BOOKS are published by Herald Press
Scottdale, Pennsylvania 15683, U.S.A.

FOR THE CHATELAINE OF
COONTAIL LAGOON

CONTENTS

1

Why This Book Was Written

This book is for wistful agnostics and reluctant atheists.

Wistful agnostics are people who want to believe in God but are held back by doubt as to whether it is intellectually respectable to do so.

Reluctant atheists have concluded God does not exist but are unhappy with that conclusion because they still feel a deep need for a source of value and meaning beyond themselves.

Wistful agnostics and reluctant atheists are very numerous today. They are particularly visible on college campuses. But if you look closely you also will find a good deal of unwilling disbelief among middle-aged parents who dutifully shepherd their children to church on Sunday. You can encounter it even among the men—doubly vulnerable to doubt because of the intense sincerity of their will to believe—who have to stand in a pulpit every week and preach a sermon.

I have a great empathy for wistful agnostics and reluctant atheists because I used to be one myself. If any demon for syntax asks, "One of which?" the answer is, both. As a young man, I was a wistful agnostic. Over the years I slid imperceptibly—as agnostics are apt to do—into active disbelief.

This increase in skepticism proved to be a great gain because it finally compelled me to undertake an intensive study of the arguments for and against God. My inquiry began with reading— hundreds of books on both sides of the question. It led at last to experimentation—the empirical testing of religious affirmations in the laboratory of my own life. And that led to this book.

I will try to convince you of three things which I now deeply believe to be true:

* * * Disbelief is widespread today, not because the evidence for God has been weighed and found wanting, but rather because all of us have been conditioned by contemporary culture to reject uncritically the whole idea of a reality transcending the natural world of physical objects and forces.

* * * When examined with an open mind, the evidence for the reality of God is very strong indeed. Although neither science nor philosophy can "prove" the existence of God, both offer cogent rational arguments for accepting theism as a plausible hypothesis.

* * * The reality of God can be tested and verified by direct personal experience. We do not have to remain hung up forever in speculations *about* God. Anyone who really wants to do so can *know* God—can have an immediate awareness of His presence that is fully as self-authenticating as any knowledge that reaches us through our five physical senses.

In the pages that follow I will quote many wise men and women whose insights have been helpful to me, in the hope they also will be helpful to you. But I won't try to snow you with an impressive array of "authorities." Whether I use my own words or those of others, what I will be trying to say to you in utmost sincerity, as one human being to another, is that *I have tried this—and it works.*

I don't ask you to take my word for it—except perhaps as a tentative working hypothesis. The decision about God is one each person must make *and test* for himself. Belief in God which consists merely of giving assent to (or refusing to acknowledge doubt about) verbal assertions of His existence is of very little value. Unless it is undergirded and validated by personal experience, it will prove to be a sandy foundation when winds blow and floodwaters rise around the walls of a human life.

For that reason, I hope you will regard the opening chapters of this book as purely preliminary—a necessary ground-clearing exercise to dispose of certain arbitrary obstacles to belief, including the widespread notion that it is irrational and unscientific. They are not intended to confront you with what philosophers call a "knockdown argument" but merely to give you enough confidence in the *possibility* of God's reality to encourage you to put it to the test for yourself.

The rest of the book suggests ways in which that can be done. If one of them doesn't seem to work for you, try another. Each of us has his own way of getting to know God. For some, the route leads through prayer and mysticism. Others encounter God in action, by obeying His command to give themselves in loving service to mankind. Many discover Him as a power, a light, a liberating joy that dwells deep within their hearts and enables them to be kinder, more loving, more hopeful, more free than they could ever be if they had to rely solely on their own strength.

It is not easy for anyone whose unconscious attitudes have been shaped by contemporary culture to arrive at a confident and serene knowledge of God. You may find your experiment beset by many difficulties, failures and frustrations. I have come in recent years to the suspicion that God deliberately hides His reality from the casual inquirer because He knows that our joy when we find Him will be directly proportional to the hunger and yearning with which we have sought Him.

As a pilgrim who has trod this path and knows how steep and rocky it can get, I wish with all my heart that I could somehow impart to you now my own hard-won certainty that it does at last lead somewhere, and that the destination makes the trip infinitely worth while. But this is a truth you must establish for yourself. And you will do so if you hang in there and don't give up too easily.

2

The Reasons For Our Unbelief

The first big hurdle every modern pilgrim must surmount is a built-in, largely unconscious bias against belief in God.

You may not be aware of having such a bias. But, as an educated person of our time, you almost certainly do, for you have been exposed, like the rest of us, to a culture-conditioning which strongly predisposes us to skepticism about the existence of an order of reality transcending nature.

Dr. Will Herberg, the great Jewish scholar who teaches philosophy at Drew University, says this brainwashing which all of us receive daily from our cultural environment is a far more important cause of contemporary atheism than any rational argument that anyone has been able to make against the idea of God.

"What has affected the modern mind," says Dr. Herberg, "has not been an array of intellectual arguments, but the unremitting operation of mind-setting attitudes, often hardly noticed, doing their remorseless work by cultural pressures and compulsions."

Another distinguished modern scholar, sociologist Peter Berger, explains why cultural attitudes can have such a coercive effect on individual beliefs.

"Most of what we 'know' is taken on the authority of others," Dr. Berger points out. "And it is only as others continue to confirm this 'knowledge' that it continues to be plausible to us. . . . Conversely, the plausibility of 'knowledge' that is not socially shared, that is challenged by our fellow men, is imperiled, not just in our dealings with others, but much more importantly in our own minds."

THE SCIENTIFIC FALLACY

In other words, it is hard to believe in God in a time, such as the present, when it is fashionable to proclaim Him dead. But to recognize that the idea of God has ceased to be credible for large numbers of men and women is a statement about the culture we live in and has no necessary bearing on the truth or falsity of the idea itself. "The reality of God is not affected by whether or not I am aware of his presence," observes Dr. Robert McAfee Brown, professor of religion at Stanford University. "The fact that I don't see the sun at any given moment doesn't mean it is not there. My eyes may be closed. There may be heavy clouds. Or I may be looking in the wrong direction."

Several different intellectual fashions have helped to create our present cultural climate and its built-in bias against belief in God. One of the most important factors, certainly, is the awe in which physical science is held by many laymen who know relatively little about actual scientific research. Every age has its superstitions, and ours is the notion that science is an infallible and all-sufficient guide to truth. The corollary is that the only kind of reality worth bothering about is that which can be verified by the methods of physical science.

Scientists, if consulted, would vigorously refute this idea. They are keenly aware that science itself depends on assumptions—such as the order and intelligibility of the natural universe—which cannot be verified by scientific methods but must be accepted, so to speak, on faith. "Science is impossible without faith—the faith that nature is subject to law," says Norbert Wiener, the father of cybernetics.

Sir William James, the pioneer pyschologist, was even more emphatic in rejecting the superstition that truth can be ascertained only through the weightings and measurings of science. "Humbug is humbug, even though it wear the scientific name," he said. "And the total expression of human experience, as I view it objectively, invincibly urges me beyond narrow 'scientific' bounds. Assuredly the real world is . . . more intricately built than physical science allows."

Despite these warnings from great scientists, large numbers of laymen cling, in the name of "science," to the idea that nothing can be real unless it can be detected, measured and analyzed by methods of physical science. And, since God is not an object, not a physical entity that can be subjected to scientific analysis, this superstition serves as a mental block to belief in God.

THE FREUDIAN MISCONCEPTION

Another widely prevalent mental block is the idea, derived from Freudian psychology, that belief in God can be explained as a wish-fulfillment projection of man's inner longing for security. The argument was expressed by Dr. Sigmund Freud in these words:

"It would indeed be very nice if there were a God, who was both creator of the world and a benevolent providence; if there were a moral world order and a future life. But at the same time it is very odd that all this is just as we should wish it ourselves."

There are two great fallacies in this argument. The first is that men naturally want to believe in God because they find it comforting. Had Freud taken a poll on this point, he would have found that many people are burdened with concepts of God that are so unpalatable they'd gladly vote for His non-existence if they had a choice in the matter.

The other fallacy in the Freudian argument is the implicit assumption that a belief *must* be illusory if it happens to satisfy our wishes. But it is equally plausible—as Freud's famous contemporary Carl Jung pointed out—to regard a widespread human yearning after God as an indication that there may lurk in the collective unconscious of the race the awareness of a reality that is not universally apprehended by conscious minds. All other basic human instincts—such as sex and hunger—find fulfillment in objective realities. Why should the faith instinct alone be viewed as a neurotic quest for what is not?

THE SECULAR CONCERN WITH THINGS

A third aspect of modern culture which militates against belief in God is our preoccupation with secular concerns. "People are just too damn busy to worry about the existence of God," said one of the most perceptive Catholic theologians of our century, Father John Courtney Murray.

Our secularity is in part a product of affluence. We are swamped by *things*, which must be bought, paid for, used, repaired, remodeled and replaced. We possess them—and are possessed by them. But our secularity is also in part the result of a nobler characteristic which is quite commonplace today, especially among young people. This is a commitment to the eradication of injustice and gross inequality in society. To say that this is a secular goal is not to suggest that it is in any way contrary to God's will—I am personally convinced that just the opposite is true. But because it focuses our attention on the here-and-now world of material needs and human interrelationships, it can be—and for many has been—a distraction from any serious consideration of the God question.

THE CREDIBILITY GAP

Still another mind-setting attitude which we derive from contemporary culture is the pervasive cynicism that has developed in response to attempts by advertisers, politicians and other hidden persuaders to massage our minds.

We've been subliminally stimulated, motivationally manipulated, erotically titillated and otherwise gulled so often that we have become like hunted animals, picking our way warily through the media jungle, knowing it to be full of cleverly hidden snares.

Our skepticism is understandable enough. But when disbelief becomes automatic reflex, as it has for many of us today, it is as poor a guide to truth as naive credulity.

"There was a time when we fooled ourselves by believing too much," said the late Dr. Ralph Sockman. "Now I think many of us are fooling ourselves by believing too little."

The credibility gap is particularly wide where the Church is concerned. This is due in part to the fact that the Church is an institution, and it is currently the mode to speak scornfully of all institutions. But it also is attributable to the Church's own failures and shortcomings.

Sometimes the Church has spoken too dogmatically, claiming certitude where a humble affirmation of faith would have been more convincing. And sometimes it has gone to the other extreme, watering down its beliefs to the point of irrelevancy in a craven and futile attempt to make them congenial to a disbelieving culture.

In its obscurantist phases, the Church has tolerated, and even encouraged, popular ideas about God which are so grossly inadequate and misleading that they can only antagonize thoughtful people who come in contact with them. In its frantic efforts to make the scene with modern man, it has spawned theological speculations so bizarre that they merely amuse non-believers (while seriously demoralizing believers).

The Church has made a further contribution to disbelief by failing to practice what it preaches. Its gospel calls upon men to be self-sacrificing in their dedication to the welfare of others. Yet the Church itself too often has seemed to be self-centered, dedicated first of all to its own institutional interests. "It may be that the major reason for unbelief in our time," says Dr. Harvey Cox, professor of divinity at Harvard University, "is not that people find the gospel incredible, but that they find the Church incredible."

NO CAPACITY FOR WONDER

Finally, contemporary culture is biased against belief in God because we have suffered atrophy of our capacity for *wonder*. In our uncritical adulation of science and our preoccupation with secular concerns, we have drifted into the habit of thinking that we live in an open-book universe where everything that happens can be explained in "natural" terms, and there are no irruptions of the mysterious, the inexplicable, the Other.

But this is *not* such a universe. From birth to death, we are surrounded by marvels—not least the shocking fact of our own existence—which should keep us in a state of continual awe.

The scientists who know most about the universe do feel this awe; it is a continually recurring theme in their literature. It is only we laymen who believe that all of the mystery went out of a flower when botanists learned to name its parts, or that a sunset ceased to carry a profound message for the human spirit when we found that its dazzling colors come from the refraction of light through dust particles in the atmosphere.

Is the birth of a baby any less wonderful because we know about sperm and ova and cell division and chromosomes? Is death any less intimidating because someone has traced the stages in which the cells of the body perish when deprived of oxygen-bearing blood?

Surely the answer is no in both cases. We need only to look at the *wholeness* of things—at the realities we actually encounter in our daily existence—to see once again, as our predecessors in the human adventure saw so clearly, that there are more things in this world than are dreamt of in *anyone's* philosophy.

3

The Inadequate Concepts
Of God

During his long career as pastor of New York's Riverside Church, the late Harry Emerson Fosdick spent many hours counseling students from nearby Columbia University. One evening a distraught young man burst into his study and announced:

"I have decided that I cannot and do not believe in God."

"All right," Dr. Fosdick replied. "But describe for me the God you don't believe in."

The student proceeded to sketch his idea of God. When he finished, Dr. Fosdick said:

"Well, we're in the same boat. I don't believe in that God either."

An amazingly large number of otherwise well-educated people seem to arrive at adulthood with concepts of God that are at best immature and at worst grotesque caricatures. This is another big hurdle impeding the modern pilgrim's progress, and the purpose of this chapter is to help you over it.

I won't even try to tell you exactly what God *is* like. I don't know—and neither does anyone else.

Any concept of deity that is within the grasp of human minds is bound to limit, and therefore distort, the infinite and incomprehensible Reality which lies behind that much-abused proper noun, "God."

If all concepts of God are inadequate, does it really matter which ones we have? Yes, it does. The experience of countless other pilgrims has demonstrated that some images and analogies do *point toward* God even though they fail to encompass Him.

Our goal in the pages that follow is to identify certain concepts of God, widely held today, that are misleading and harmful, and to suggest alternative images and analogies that are more valid and useful as road markers on your way to direct personal encounter with God.

THE SUPREME BEING

First, let's examine the idea that God is "the Supreme Being." Its popularity is attested by long-continued usage. It was George Washington's favorite term for deity, and we still find it used in good dictionaries to define the meaning of the word "God."

The trouble with this ancient phrase is that it automatically steers our thoughts about God into the categories of Greek philosophy, particularly the teachings of Aristotle, which tend to equate reality with "substance." Aristotle had his own special meaning for this word, but however subtle his definitions he never managed to purge it entirely of spatial connotations. If God is "the Supreme Being," then He is *a* being, and in Aristotelian philosophy, which has been the intellectual matrix of

Christian theology since the time of St. Thomas Aquinas, a being must have substance.

Aquinas knew, and all subsequent theological students have been taught, that the "substance" of God is spiritual and therefore cannot be thought of in the same way as the substance of a material object that can be weighed, touched, measured and located in space. But this crucial distinction has never gotten through to the vast majority of laymen (nor, I sometimes think, to many clergymen).

The result is that a lot of people think of God as existing at some specific spatial location "up there" or "out there."

This is, of course, utter nonsense. In the space age belief in such a God can be retained only by checking your brains at the church door. But we did not have to wait for the era of extraterrestrial travel to discover how absurd it is to attribute spatial location to the author of the universe. Two thousand years ago a Palestinian carpenter named Jesus was explaining to his disciples that "God is Spirit," dwelling not on the tops of sacred mountains nor in the sanctums of temples, but in the hearts of men.

In recent years several able theologians, including Paul Tillich, Leslie Dewart and Nels Ferré, have sought to rescue the concept of God from what Ferré calls "the dungeon of Greek philosophy."

Professor Ferré wishes we'd all forget that phrase "Supreme Being."

"If God is a being, he is somewhere," says Ferré. And if He can be localized, then He is a "thing"— that is, He has the quality of material objectivity which is proper to things.

To shock people out of this pattern of thought,

Ferré is fond of saying that "God is nowhere and nothing"—which, if you insert hyphens in the right places, is precisely what Jesus taught. God is no-where because His reality transcends space, and He is no-thing because His reality transcends that of an object.

Professor Dewart carries the shock treatment a step further by stating blandly that "God does not exist." He explains that "existence" is a term which can properly be applied only to persons or things that have *come into being*, whose reality is contingent on something that happened but need not necessarily have happened.

"To attribute existence to God is the most extreme form of anthropomorphism," says Dewart. "What the religious experience of God discloses is a Reality beyond being."

But it was the great Paul Tillich who most eloquently protested the term "Supreme Being" and all talk of God's "existence."

God is not a being among other beings, Tillich said, "He is being-itself beyond essence and existence. To argue that God 'exists' is to deny him."

He is not "an object within reality, but the matrix of reality."

He is "the answer to the question implied in the fact that there are beings and objects that exist"—the reason why there is something instead of nothing.

It is a striking fact—although, so far as I know, Tillich himself never pointed it out—that his metaphors for God have a great affinity with the name which the ancient Hebrews used for God—YHWH (pronounced Yahweh), "He causes to be."

Although the thought of men like Tillich, Dewart and Ferré has helped to restore the concept of God to the high intellectual plane on which God-talk took place before Aristotle got into the act, many intensely modern people have difficulty wrapping their minds around such abstractions as "being itself." Another contemporary theologian, John B. Cobb, Jr., suggests an analogy that may be helpful in learning to think of God as an illimitable Presence rather than a spatially located object.

"Suppose we are listening to stereophonic music in a dark room. Is the music an object? That is hardly a useful category. It can neither be seen nor touched, and it cannot be located as being at some one place. It 'fills' the room and may simultaneously 'fill' many other rooms as well. It is profoundly subjective in that it stirs our depths and permeates our whole experience. Yet it is profoundly objective in that it comes to us from without and has a pattern we do not determine.

"I do not mean to suggest that music is a particularly good model for thinking about God. I want only to indicate that the world given us in hearing is neither a world of objects nor wholly non-objective and beyond conceptualization.

"The presence of God is much more like the presence of music than like that of a rock or a machine. It is like that of music in being intensely subjective. But like music it is also objective in that it comes to us from beyond our own being and determination."

THE PERSONAL GOD

Another bit of traditional terminology that has bred enormous confusion is the custom of referring to God as a person.

Here, as in the case of "Supreme Being," the basic difficulty stems from the anthropomorphic images which the word "person" inevitably raises in people's minds. When they are asked to believe in "a personal God," they immediately start thinking in terms of a very big man.

This is obviously a childish and untenable concept of deity. Yet it retains a large following, especially among atheists, who find it an easy target. No idea of God is so easy to deny or laugh out of court as this one.

The difficulty is compounded when people go on—as many do—to fill in their mental picture with details of the *kind* of extra-large man they think God is.

Two images seem to dominate popular imagination. One is that of the Great Scorekeeper in the Sky, a harsh, unloving and unlovable Fellow who lays down strict rules, knowing His human creatures cannot keep them, and gleefully marks up each transgression, awaiting the day when He can subject them to brutal and unremitting punishment.

Abbé Louis Evely, who has done so much to revive the life of the spirit in the Roman Catholic Church, says he was brought up to think of God as this kind of "inexorable Judge." This type of religious teaching is, tragically, still quite common in many Protestant denominations as well as the Catholic Church. And, as Abbé Evely points out, "the only result is to prevent man from ever loving God."

Why Christian bodies permit and sometimes even encourage the promulgation of such an image is a mystery, because it not only is highly uncomplimentary to God, it also is directly contradictory of everything that Jesus Christ taught about the loving, forgiving, accepting, ever merciful nature of God.

At the opposite end of the spectrum of anthropomorphic images is the conception of God as Our Grandfather in Heaven.

That this conception has acquired a tremendous following in modern America is hardly surprising. It comforts people who are enjoying the benefits of an affluent society and would like to believe that their luxuries are the just reward for their virtues and a token of God's complete satisfaction with their way of life.

Wherever this view of God may have come from, it cannot fairly be blamed on the Bible. The Bible tells over and over again of good men who suffered for serving God, and of wicked men who prospered. In the New Testament we find Jesus using the image of a loving father to convey a sense of God's disposition toward human creatures. In the Jewish homes of first-century Palestine the father was not an ineffectual, overindulgent soft touch. He was the benevolent but undisputed ruler of the household, and was far more concerned with the spiritual welfare and growth of his children than with insuring them instant access to every creature comfort they might desire.

If the concept of a personal God leads to such aberrations, should we not abandon it entirely and think of God solely in abstract terms such as "Ground of Being" or "Ultimate Reality"?

I think not—although I readily admit a case may be made for the change. As soon as we begin referring to God as "It" rather than as "He," we are apt to stumble into an even deeper pitfall. *Personality*—willing, purposing, caring, communicating personality—is the highest and most complex category of reality that we human beings have discovered in the universe. We may, indeed must, assume that God's reality infinitely transcends personality as we know it, but we certainly have no warrant for thinking that it can be expressed in any lesser category.

To speak of God as a person may be inadequate and misleading. But to speak of God as a thing (even such an impressive-sounding thing as a "cosmic force") is insulting.

Moreover, as Leslie Dewart points out, "God's relations with man are necessarily personal, for *we* are persons." A flower or a stone or a star may experience God as an impersonal force, but men experience God as "Thou."

It has been pointed out often—too often, in my opinion—that men *want* to think of God as a person because they find it impossible to pray to or trust in a "cosmic force." But this is an observation about men and does not necessarily say anything about God. The important thing, I believe, is not that men yearn for a sense of personal relationship with the Source of Being, but that some men, actually quite a large number over the centuries, have had experiences which they are able to describe only in terms of an intensely personal relationship with a Reality that does such *person-like* things as loving, demanding, forgiving, and persuading. On the basis of this evidence, even such rigorously scientific thinkers as William James and Alfred North Whitehead were prepared to use personal nouns such as "Friend" and "Companion" in speaking of God.*

GOD OF THE GAPS

Another popular concept of God, which has often proved a short cut to atheism, developed as a defensive reaction against the advance of scientific knowledge.

Men have always tended to use "God" as a hypothesis to explain what they otherwise find inexplicable. Thus the ancient Greeks, for all of their sophistication, made free use of their overpopulated pantheon to account for events such as earthquakes and eclipses, which their science had not yet learned to explain in terms of natural causes.

The advance of scientific understanding proceeded very slowly for many centuries, but since the eighteenth century, and particularly in our own century, it has been very swift indeed. And the more man has learned about nature, the less need he has felt to invoke God in the role of Celestial Magician.

Sad to say, some theologians, a good many clergymen and a great many laymen, who should have

*Sharp-eyed readers will already have observed that I've used personal pronouns in reference to God throughout this book. I did so, despite misgivings about their effect in reinforcing anthropomorphic concepts of God, because the English language offers only two other alternatives: (1) sidestep the problem by repeating the proper noun in every case, which makes for a stiff and awkward style of writing; or (2) use the impersonal pronoun "It," which seems to me even less appropriate and more misleading in its connotations than "He" or "Him." Before militant feminists take up arms, let me hasten to acknowledge that "She" also is a theoretical possibility. But I did not consider it a serious alternative because "He" has long been accepted usage as an all-purpose personal pronoun in situations where gender is not a relevant consideration.

welcomed this development, instead were plunged into panic. They embarked on a frantic effort to find gaps and flaws in the chain of causality in nature, into which God could be reintroduced.

Germany's martyr-theologian of World War II, Dietrich Bonhoeffer, warned his fellow Christians, shortly before his death on a Nazi scaffold, that it was foolish and wrong "to use God as a stopgap for the incompleteness of our knowledge.

"We should find God in what we do know, not what we don't know," Bonhoeffer wrote from his prison cell.

Seeking God in the gaps is doubly absurd because it is so patently unnecessary. A mature concept of God finds no threat in any scientific discovery, for it views God—in perfect fidelity to the Bible—as the creative principle at work in all operations of nature and in all human achievements. In the vivid metaphor of C.S. Lewis, God is not "a player who strolls on the stage occasionally to bring off some startling effect" but is "the author and director of the whole show."

THE OMNIPOTENT GOD

In their unflagging determination to diagram God, medieval scholastics began with the premise that He is a "perfect being," and went on from there to list the various attributes such a being must possess. By this process they arrived at what has proved to be one of the most disastrous of all ideas about God—namely, the belief that He is omnipotent, or all-powerful.

To most people, omnipotence means, "God can do anything He wants." In other words, God is thought of as an oriental sultan whose domain is universal and whose reign is eternal.

This is a disastrous concept because it lands theism in a quandary which probably has driven more thoughtful people to atheism than any other one thing—the so-called "problem of evil." The problem is this:

If a good and all-powerful God created the world, why is it so full of evil?

Christian apologists have writhed on the point of that sharp question for centuries, and have come up with some marvelously ingenious answers. But their answers have been unconvincing to a great many people, who find more logic in the famous statement of the philosopher John Stuart Mill:

"If God is able to prevent evil and does not, he is not good. If he would prevent evil and cannot, he is not almighty."

It is not merely the intellect but, even more, the heart that rebels against belief in a God who would deliberately inflict the vast amount of pain and misery that besets man and his fellow creatures. A modern poet, Robert Hale, has eloquently expressed the virtual impossibility of loving such a God:

> If you give me a choice
> between voting for
> "God is dead"
>   or
> "Everything (including evil) is God's will,"
> I would have to abstain.

Happily, the choice does not lie between those bleak alternatives, and this has been made clear by modern theologians such as Charles Hartshorne, Norman Pittenger, and John B. Cobb, Jr.

They point out two major fallacies in the traditional doctrine of omnipotence. It ignores the radical freedom which manifestly exists at every level of the universe, from the random movement of electrons to the darting thoughts of the human mind. And it attributes the wrong kind of power to God.

Believers are as mistaken in attributing everything that happens to God as atheists are in attributing everything to blind chance, says Hartshorne. Both "Providence"—the will of God—and chance are operative in the world.

"The details of events—and our sufferings are among the details—are not contrived, or planned, or divinely decreed. They just happen—period. What *is* decreed is that it shall be possible for them to happen, but also possible for other, and partly better, things to happen."

But why does God bestow such a large degree of freedom upon the universe and its inhabitants? Why didn't He create a world in which nature would always be benign and men would necessarily be good and kind and peaceful?

Because, Hartshorne says, "the creaturely freedom from which evils spring is also an essential aspect of all goods, so that the price of a guaranteed absence of evil would be the equally guaranteed absence of good."

In other words, if there were no freedom, there would be no virtue. If man were merely a talking puppet manipulated by a divine wire puller, he could do no wrong, but neither could he do any good. Were there no opportunity to be selfish, craven, dishonest or hateful, it would be meaningless to speak of being unselfish, brave, truthful and loving.

Developing Hartshorne's theme, Cobb asserts that it is "profoundly blasphemous" to hold God responsible for everything that happens, just as it happens.

"If this is taken at face value, God is the cause not only of destructive earthquakes and plagues, but also of human sin. If he then holds man accountable for these sins, God is worthy of moral contempt, and the brave man would be called to rebellion, however futile."

The basic trouble with the whole concept of omnipotence, Cobb says, is that it is usually taken to mean that there is only one power, namely God, and that all else is wholly powerless.

But this idea that God has a monopoly of power is foreign to the Bible, which depicts God as being engaged in a constant struggle to maximize the good and minimize the evil in a world in which His will can be and quite often is defied.

Moreover, the doctrine of omnipotence assumes that God's power is "the power to compel or force." And this is "a wretched and pitiful form of power" which even a human parent should disdain to use in dealing with his children, except as a last resort.

The New Testament offers a clue to the real nature of God's power. It is not the power to compel, but rather "the kind of power exercised by a wise and effective parent—the power of persuasion."

Pittenger sees God as "the chief, but not the only, explanation of how things go in the world."

"He is the living, dynamic personal Love who is ever at work to establish in the world more love and goodness, hence more justice and righteousness." But it is profoundly unbiblical, and contrary to all religious experience, to think of Him as a "despotic ruler."

"A much better model," says Pittenger, "would be the man whose character is sheer goodness, who is always faithful to his purpose and loyal to his friends, who 'lets them be' but is affected by what they think and do, and who yet has enough resources of love to adapt himself to new circumstances and situations, and to make the best that can conceivably be made of them.

"That, I suggest, is the sort of model which makes sense of God in the world we live in. It is a world in which there is chance, there is risk, there is recalcitrance. Yet goodness is known, truth is obtainable, beauty is present within that world—and above all, love is experienced there. God is not the *only* explanation of it, since there is a radical freedom in the world, straight down to the minutest bit of energy and straight up to man's capacity to accept or refuse the best that is available to him; hence creaturely Yes and creaturely No play their part in explaining how things are. But chief among all the decisions is the decision made by the 'pure unbounded Love' which is God. The world does show a pattern, and as scientists increasingly affirm, the pattern is one of ceaselessly renewed and ever more integrated occasions for the expression of good."

Hartshorne, Cobb and Pittenger are Protestant theologians. Their thinking about God is shared by a Catholic theologian, Father Avery Dulles, S.J., and an eminent biologist who also is a religious philosopher, Dr. L. Charles Birch.

Father Dulles says images which depict men as God's puppets are directly contradictory to the New Testament, which insists over and over again that men are not slaves but are freemen, friends and sons of God.

"We must cease to look on God as a kind of authority figure standing over against man. Our dominant God-image should be that of one who loves and gives himself to man. Love does not enslave the other or impede his development. It brings out his highest potentialities. Love is the key to freedom without selfishness, service without enslavement."

Dr. Birch, in a superb little book entitled *Nature and God*, says that neither science nor true religion can accept the idea that God exercises "dictatorial, coercive power" over the world. The divine influence that *can* be discerned in the world is "the power of persuasive love." And there are important corollaries to this:

"If all God's activity is in the nature of persuasive love, there must be room in the universe for spontaneity of response, a degree of self-determination on the part of the creature, and room for the accidental and unpredictable.

"The purposes of God in creation are not implemented as a series of arbitrary acts, but as a struggle between a disordered state and God's lure to completeness. In this view, cosmic evolution involves a fighting frontier of persuasive love in a universe that contains an anarchic element. . . . At each stage [of the continual creative process called evolution] God confronts what is actual in the world with what is possible for it."

But why does not God speed up the process and bring the universe to perfection all at once instead of waiting billions of years for it to evolve into what He purposes it to be?

"Because he is a God of creation and not a magician. At each stage of the creative process, there are limitations on what can be actualized in the immediate future. The opportunities are limited by what has already been achieved. . . . This is the cost of creation. For God to control the world completely, to take away its freedom and spontaneity, would be to destroy it."

But freedom, if it is to be genuine, necessarily "involves the possibilities of imperfection and disorder. . . . Where there is freedom, there is also the possibility of tragedy. To ask for anything else is to ask for an irresistible might in complete control of all details. This might be a man's idea of what a power-God could do. But it is not what a God of love would do. And it does not happen."

And is the price too high? Would it really be better to live in a playpen world from which all possibility of deliberate evil or accidental pain had been banished?

The great South African novelist Alan Paton, no stranger to evil or pain, thinks not. Confessing his distaste for pollyanna talk about the ennobling effects of suffering, Paton says that his experience of life has led him to the intuition that it may be a necessary ingredient of a truly good world. Paton writes:

"All who are mature, whether young or old, accept suffering as inseparable from life; even when it is not experienced, the possibility of it is always there. I myself cannot conceive of life without suffering. I cannot even conceive that life would have meaning without suffering. There would be no music, no theatre, no literature, no art.

"I suspect that the alternative to a universe in which there is suffering, in which evil struggles with good and cruelty with mercy, would be a universe of nothingness, where there would be neither good nor evil, no happiness, only an eternity of uninterrupted banality.

"If my suspicion is true, then I vote for the universe we have, where we have our joy that has been made real by our suffering, as the silence of the night is made real by the sounds of the night. . . .

"Such a multifold universe, such a multifold life, despite all the unanswerable questions they raise, seem more consonant with the idea of a creative and imaginative God than any garden of Eden."

THE UNCHANGING GOD

Medieval philosophers, with their passion for ascribing absolute qualities to God, are responsible for yet another insulting idea about Him that is still widely held. This is the notion that God is unaffected by what goes on in the world.

The technical theological term for this alleged attribute of God is "impassibility." The scholastics added it to their list of divine traits in the belief that it would detract from God's glory to admit the possibility that He might be harmed in any way by anything that men do.

Actually, it was the scholastics themselves who detracted from God's glory—and ignored the plain teaching of the Bible—by imputing to God a detachment from the world's suffering that would be considered callous and despicable even in a human being.

The whole point of the Christian gospel is that God *loves* the world. And of course, to love means to care, to suffer with those who suffer, rejoice with those who rejoice, to delight in triumphs and commiserate with failures.

The same theologians who have demolished the concept of omnipotence are trying to redeem the good name of God from this libel of impassibility.

Taking their cue from Alfred North Whitehead, the most creative philosopher of the scientific era, they assert that reality is never static, but always in the process of changing. And God is not only the author of the process: He is Himself involved in it.

In other words, God, like the universe, both *is* and is in the process of *becoming*.

Far from being unchangeable and unaffected by the events of the world, the process theologians say, God is constantly interacting with the world, influencing it by the power of persuasive love and at the same time being influenced by it.

Some critics fear that this sort of thinking may lead toward pantheism, in which God becomes simply synonymous with the universe. But Whitehead's interpreters insist that their view is not pantheistic, but rather panentheistic, upholding both the "immanence" of God as a creative power at work within nature and His "transcendence" as a Reality utterly beyond, above, other than and independent of the world of matter and energy.

This modern concept of a "living and growing God" has been developed most radically by Schubert M. Ogden, one of the early exponents of process theology.

"Because God himself is most immediately affected by all that we are and do, the future for which we live our lives is neither merely our own nor that of others as limited as ourselves, but also the unending future of God's own becoming, in which we are given to share. It is God's self-creation that is the ultimate cause advanced or retarded by all our lesser causes and their issues; and the motive finally inspiring our own decisions as men, in relation to one another and to all our fellow creatures, is so to maximize the being and joy of the world as to increase as fully as we can the concrete perfection of God's everlasting life."

John B. Cobb, Jr., says that process theology is simply taking seriously the truth which is symbolized in the New Testament by the cross of Christ —that "God shares with us in the suffering that accompanies the existence he has given us." In Whitehead's words, "God is the Great Companion —the fellow-sufferer who understands."

This concept of God not only makes men responsible for the future: it also is man's best ground for a serene facing of the future. If all the experiences of humanity are retained forever as an imprint on the nature of God, "neither individual death nor the extinction of the human race will be so total a loss as it otherwise appears.

"Even our little virtues and petty triumphs are not ultimately in vain. And perhaps even our meaningless suffering can be subsumed into a large meaning within the divine fire. If all we do contributes everlastingly to God, otherwise ephemeral values take on importance" and no good purpose, no loving thought, no kind deed and, above all, no life is ever wasted.

4

Why Do We Exist?

Once you've found a concept of God that you'd *like* to believe in, your next question is whether it is *possible* for a rational and intelligent person to believe in the reality of God.

I contend that it is. In fact, I will argue in this chapter that belief in God is the *only* hypothesis that can satisfy two of man's most fundamental instincts: the drive to understand and the need for meaning.

The desire to make sense out of the world is a distinctive human trait not shared by other animals. A cat or dog may display curiosity about a specific object or event. But man's quest for comprehension goes far beyond mere curiosity. He wants to know *why* things are as they are. He gropes for relationships, seeks to identify causes and effects. He often has to settle for partial explanations but is never fully satisfied with them.

As long as Man the Inquirer focuses his attention on secondary causes, he is neither inhibited nor helped by a philosophy that excludes God. But the drive to understand leads eventually to what

Paul Tillich called "the riddle of all riddles—the mystery that there is anything at all."

We are so accustomed to taking the universe for granted, it startles us to realize that it might have been otherwise. Yet anyone who ponders the matter for a moment must see that there is no necessary reason for the existence of the world or anything in it.

Atheism cannot, and in fact does not attempt to, provide any clue to the riddle of why there is something instead of nothing. Its stand on the question was brusquely summed up by Bertrand Russell: "The universe is just there, that's all."

But to settle for a senseless universe seems a strange piece of defeatism for men of scientific age. And if your intuition insists that there must be *some* reason for the existence of the universe, you will discover there is only one sufficient postulate on the market. It is the one given in the opening words of the Bible: "In the beginning, God created . . ."

THE SOURCE OF BEING

The great philosopher of the Middle Ages, St. Thomas Aquinas, laid down the basic principle, which is just as logical and scientifically valid today as it was then: "That which does not exist can begin to exist only through something already existing."

This means that the continuous chain of causation, which science has found to be operative in the natural world, must lead ultimately to something whose existence is not contingent but necessary; not derived but original; not caused but causing: in short to a Source of Being, or God.

The difficulty with all philosophical arguments which seek to establish God as a logical necessity is that the people they're supposed to convince usually find it at least as hard to conceive of a self-existent God as to conceive of a self-existent universe. I must confess that I don't have this problem. To me, the concept of a self-existent God seems entirely plausible, while the idea that the universe is "just there" repels my intellect. But I recognize that this is purely an intuitive response, and therefore highly personal. I don't expect anyone else to accept it just because I do. So if the argument-from-the-cosmos leaves you unpersuaded, forget it and let's begin instead with a fact on which everyone can agree: for some reason, the universe *is* here. Through science and observation, man has learned a good bit about it. The question is, which hypothesis—atheism or belief in God—is more compatible with the observed phenomena?

The assumption that atheism is more "scientific" than belief in God is very widely held today, as a result of the mind-setting attitudes of contemporary culture which we discussed in Chapter II. But it is an invalid assumption, repudiated by many prominent scientists.

The deeper scientists probe into the origin and evolution of life, the more reluctant they become to attribute the patterns they observe to the operation of blind chance.

"The probability of life originating from accident is comparable to the probability of the unabridged dictionary resulting from an explosion in a printing shop," says biologist Edwin Conklin.

A noted French biophysicist, Pierre LeComte du Nouy, has calculated the actual mathematical odds against the spontaneous appearance of life in a universe governed solely by chance. First, he says, it would be necessary for accidental collisions of atoms to produce protein molecules, which are essential elements of all living things. Protein molecules are large, complex and highly dissymmetrical.

"The probability for a *single* protein molecule to be formed by the action of chance and normal thermic agitation is practically nil," du Nouy says. "If we suppose 500 trillion shakings per second, which corresponds to the order of magnitude of light frequencies, we find that the time needed to form, on an average, one such molecule in a material volume equal to that of our planet is about 10^{243} billions of years (1 followed by 243 zeros)."

Of course, du Nouy goes on, the rare configuration would not necessarily appear at the *end* of the long series of shakings. It conceivably could occur right at the start. But "one molecule is of no use. Hundreds of millions of *identical* molecules are necessary" to make possible the spontaneous appearance of life. And the odds against each successive molecule turning up increase in accordance with the laws of compound probability. Thus, "if the probability of appearance of a living cell could be expressed mathematically, the preceding figures would seem negligible."

Some scientists have disputed du Nouy's calculations, arguing that he fails to give adequate weight to the possibility that conditions especially propitious for the appearance of life may have existed at some distant point in the earth's history, owing to a particularly fortuitous arrangement of the elements needed to produce a protein molecule. But this argument comes perilously close to invoking that most unscientific concept, anti-chance. And it really does not affect the force of du Nouy's

argument. Whether we postulate an incredibly un-
likely series of accidents, or the sudden appearance
of extraordinarily favorable circumstances, we are
left with the feeling, as physiologist Andrew Con-
way Ivy puts it, that "Someone must have loaded
the dice."

Or at least *I* am left with that feeling. Perhaps
you are not. If so, waive the point. Let's assume,
for the sake of argument, that life *did* appear on
earth purely by chance. We are now left with the
problem of explaining the course it has taken since
the first living organism just happened to happen.

THE MIND BEHIND EVOLUTION

In hindsight, it seems ironic that the discovery
of evolution should once have been regarded as a
severe blow at theistic belief. For the findings of
science about the evolutionary process constitute
one of the strongest arguments for the hypothesis
that there is a creative mind and will at work in
the universe.

Professor Claude Tresmontant, lecturer on the
philosophy of science at the Sorbonne University
in Paris, goes so far as to suggest that the growing
body of scientific knowledge about evolution has
made atheism an intellectually untenable position.

Those who would deny God, he says, must be
prepared to affirm that mindless, inanimate matter
"has been able to organize itself, to become ani-
mated, and to endow itself with consciousness and
thought.

"If matter is to be looked at in this way, it has
to be credited with very great resources. For matter to have been able, on its own, to invent bio-
logical evolution, which constantly has tended

throughout the ages toward the creation of ever more complex and differentiated organisms, endowed with bigger brains and ever greater degree of consciousness, it must be gifted with great resources. In fact, it must be credited with all the attributes that theologians specify as belonging to God."

Pierre Teilhard de Chardin, the great French paleontologist-priest who devoted his life to working out a synthesis of scientific and religious thought, also found in the facts of evolution irresistible testimony to the operation of a divine Purpose.

If we had to reckon only with mindless matter, Teilhard said, we should expect it to obey the second law of thermodynamics, which affirms a universal trend toward the equal distribution of energy throughout all space. The logical result of the unchecked operation of this law would be a gradual decay of all complex organisms toward simpler and less differentiated states.

But what we actually observe in the universe is exactly the reverse: a process of "complexification," going on for billions of years, moving from inanimate matter to living organisms, evolving ever higher forms of life, and finally bringing forth the supremely improbably phenomenon of man, a creature endowed with the capacity for self-consciousness, reflective thought and the exercise of will.

It is not only the upward direction of evolution that defies explanation by the laws of probability. It is equally impossible to account, within a purely materialistic world view, for the basic hospitality of the natural environment toward life. This is a world in which life has been able to emerge, flourish and persist, and it is very hard to believe that such a world could just happen. Those who have more than a speaking acquaintance with the life sciences find their minds reeling when they think of all the favorable circumstances which must coincide at every moment if any living thing is to survive.

THE SENSE OF MORAL OBLIGATION

Another form of this argument-from-design seizes upon the one achievement of evolution which would be most improbable if the world were purely the product of blind chance. In the very act of reading this sentence, you are demonstrating the achievement, which is a capacity for *thought*.

"The emergence of even the simplest mind from no mind at all seems, to me at least, utterly incomprehensible," says biologist Sewall Wright.

Still another intimation of the reality of God can be found in the sense of absolute obligation which all of us sometimes experience.

Efforts have been made to explain man's moral consciousness as merely an interiorization of ancient taboos and rules laid down for the preservation of society. And this is valid enough, up to a point.

"Much of the moral experience of men can be explained as the result of the necessities of social survival pressing upon the individual," says theologian John C. Bennett. "But it is not possible in this way to explain the conscience of the individual who chooses to oppose the society that surrounds him at cost to himself." Socrates drinking hemlock, Christ on the cross, an American youth who goes to jail rather than go to war refute any attempt to equate morality with social conformity.

THE RUSSELL-COPLESTON DEBATE

The crucial question is whether our sense of right and wrong is derived from universal, objective values or is merely a projection of individual, subjective feelings. This question figured in a famous debate which took place in London in 1948 between Bertrand Russell, representing the atheist view, and Father F. C. Copleston, a Jesuit priest and professor of philosophy.

Copleston argued that man's perception of values and consciousness of moral law "are best explained through the hypothesis of a transcendent Ground of value and of an Author of the moral law."

Russell insisted that the moral sense is purely subjective. "I feel that some things are good and that other things are bad. I love the things that I think are good, and I hate the things that I think are bad."

The following exchange then took place:

COPLESTON: Well, let's take the behavior of the Commandant of Belsen.* That appears to you as undesirable and evil, and to me, too. But to Adolf Hitler we suppose it appeared as something good and desirable. I suppose you'd have to admit that for Hitler it was good and for you it is evil.

RUSSELL: No, I shouldn't go quite as far as that. I mean, I think people can make mistakes in that as they can in other things. . . .

COPLESTON: But can you make a mistake if it's simply a question of reference to a feeling or emo-

*Belsen was a Nazi concentration camp at which hundreds of thousands of Jews were murdered during World War II.

tion? Surely Hitler would be the only possible judge of what appealed to his emotions. . . . If there's no objective criterion outside feeling what grounds do we have for condemning the conduct of the Commandant of Belsen?

Russell and Copleston agreed that the distinguishing characteristic of man's moral sense is that it makes him feel he "ought" to do something, whether he wants to or not. If man is merely the result of "an accidental collocation of atoms," Copleston asked, whence comes this feeling of obligation to do things contrary to his desires and often to his own best interests?

RUSSELL: I think the sense of "ought" is the effect of somebody's imagined disapproval . . . it may be God's imagined disapproval, but it's somebody's imagined disapproval. I think that is what is meant by "ought."

COPLESTON: It seems to me to be the external customs and taboos and things of that sort which can most easily be explained simply through environment and education. But all that seems to me to belong to what I call the matter of the moral law, the content. The idea of "ought," as such, can never be conveyed to a man by the tribal chief or by anybody else, because there are no other terms in which it can be conveyed.

Copleston's point was that the details of a moral code—the specific things that are held to be right and wrong—may and do vary considerably from one society to another and from one age to another. What remains constant, and what is inexplicable within a materialist world view, is the sense of "ought" itself, the recognition that some duty or obligation may have a higher claim than desire or self-interest, which has existed among the vast majority of human beings at all times and in all places.

THE SENSE OF BEAUTY

When we look inward at ourselves instead of outward at the stars, we discover another distinctive human attribute which seems to intimate that there is more to the world than dumb matter and blind chance. This is our aesthetic sense, the capacity to appreciate beauty.

Like the moral sense, the aesthetic sense is much more highly developed in some people than in others, and there are a few unfortunate folk who seem to be pathologically deprived of both. But the overwhelming majority of men do respond in some degree to beauty, not only that which is created by human effort, such as music and art, but also and especially that which we see in nature.

Go into the woods on a crisp autumn day, when the sky is an inverted Wedgwood bowl, its azure specked out with white puffs of cloud. Look at the blood-red leaves and berries of the dogwood, the oaks resplendent in burnished bronze, the profligate maples—not content with a single color— flaunting a whole palette of green, yellow, gold and scarlet.

Botanists can explain all of the natural processes which yield these dazzling effects. No "miracle" is involved—unless you count it the greatest of miracles that there should be beings like you who look upon these things and find them beautiful.

Sheer accident doubtless would produce a certain amount of beauty in a universe that consisted solely of mindless matter. But persistent and abundant beauty, unnecessary beauty that has no practical function, beauty that speaks to the part of a man which lies deeper than words or conscious thoughts can penetrate—does not this suggest there may be, behind the natural processes, an Artist who creates beauty for its own sake?

And if men are able to recognize and respond to the beauty of the Artist's creation, is it really so farfetched to believe that they may enter into other forms of mind-to-mind, spirit-to-spirit communication with Him?

MAN'S SEARCH FOR MEANING

Thus far in this chapter I've been trying to suggest some of the ways in which we are led toward belief in God by our drive to understand. Now let's consider an equally basic and universal human trait: the need for meaning.

"Ever more frequently, psychoanalysts are confronted with a new type of neurosis," says Dr. Viktor E. Frankl, professor of psychiatry at the University of Vienna. "It is characterized by loss of interest and lack of initiative. The patients crowding our clinics complain of an inner emptiness, a sense of total and ultimate meaninglessness of life."

Dr. Frankl has labeled this condition "the existential vacuum." It results, he says, from frustration of man's "inherent tendency to reach out for meanings to fulfill and values to actualize."

Man's search for meaning cannot be satisfied with values which he has ordained for himself. Invented values do not have the challenging and demanding character of values which we believe to be "given" and sanctioned by a power greater than ourselves.

A person who is convinced that his life has meaning—a meaning which comes from beyond himself—can accept much suffering and cheerfully endure great sacrifice. But without a sense of purpose, without a goal larger than the gratification of selfish desires, we can hardly endure even a life of ease and affluence. We quickly become bored with self-indulgence, and begin a frantic quest for new kicks in sex, alcohol or drugs. The quest sometimes ends in suicide—which may be, as Albert Camus intimated, the most logical solution to a meaningless existence.

Not only psychiatrists but also poets and novelists have sensed the desperate frustration of modern man trying to make it on his own in a world devoid of transcendent values that can give meaning to the ordeal of existence.

In *The Ski Bum*, novelist Romain Gary has an older man tell a restless and alienated young person:

"Your generation is suffering from what for lack of a better word I shall call *over-debunk*. There was a lot of debunking that had to be done, of course. Bigotry, militarism, nationalism, religious intolerance, hypocrisy, phoniness, all sorts of dangerous, ready-made, artificially preserved false values. But your generation and the generation before yours went too far with their debunking job. You went overboard. . . . You were so angry with all the dangerous, phony piper's tunes that you ended up by breaking all the pipes and hating all the tunes. You have reduced the world to a spiritual shambles. God is ha-ha-ha. The soul is ho-ho-ho. Booze is reality. Love is sex. . . .

"But you don't seem to enjoy it. Something is

still missing, eh? You got rid of God and, isn't that funny, something is still missing. . . ."

That eminently honest atheist, Jean Paul Sartre, readily acknowledges that a world without God is necessarily a "forlorn" world bereft of ultimate meaning.

"The existentialist finds it very distressing that God does not exist," says Sartre, "because all possibility of finding values in a heaven of ideas disappears along with Him. There can no longer be an *a priori* Good, since there is no infinite and perfect consciousness to think it. . . . Everything is permissible if God does not exist, and as a result man is forlorn, because neither within him nor without does he find anything to cling to."

Other perceptive thinkers have pointed out that atheism, when it becomes as widely prevalent as it has in our day, has a demoralizing impact on society as well as on the individual psyche.

In the fall of 1969 a group of forty Nobel Prize winners—including some of the world's most eminent physical and social scientists—assembled in Stockholm for a five-day symposium on "The Place of Value in a World of Facts." It was their consensus that civilization is gravely imperiled by the disappearance from contemporary consciousness of axiomatic, transcendent values.

Writer Arthur Koestler bluntly accused the physical scientists of bringing about the crisis by treating man as though he were "nothing but a complex biochemical mechanism."

"Keep telling a man that he is nothing but an oversized rat, and he will grow whiskers and bite your fingers," Koestler warned.

Another Nobel laureate, Harvard biologist George Wald, put it even more strongly:

"The only way the world is going to stop short of the brink of nuclear holocaust is a return to God."

Dr. Wald conceded that it may sound like "the sheerest non-academic sentimentality" to say that faith, hope and love are not merely desirable but indispensable to human survival. "But I'm convinced that this is the only way we are going to prevent the total chaos we're headed for."

GOD WITHIN OURSELVES

This basic and most important fact—that men *need* God in order to make sense of their lives—is understood intuitively, I believe, by many college students and other young people today. Most of them have little interest in institutional religion as such, but they have a great yearning for something that will provide a context for their lives and help them understand who they are, what they may become, which values are worthy of their loyalty. Although they may never use the name of God, they are seeking Him with far greater sincerity and urgency than many conventionally pious types who throw God a bone of attention by showing up in church every Sunday.

And some of these young seekers—a steadily growing number, I dare to believe—are finding God, not in dogmas and rituals, but in the innermost depths of their own being, which is and always has been the best place to look for Him.

One of the many things for which we are all indebted to this fiercely honest young generation is rediscovery of a fact which the early Christian community considered the most basic support of its faith: the fact that God is not merely an idea to be believed in and talked about, but also a Reality to be encountered, experienced, known and loved.

In the next few chapters we'll consider some of the places where you can expect to encounter God and some of the ways in which you can experience His presence in your own life.

5

Jesus As Your Guide

Once there was a young man who wore sandals, a beard and long hair.

His parents were law-abiding, middle-class folks. They provided a good home for their son, sent him to the right schools and took him to worship services every Sabbath. They expected that someday he would take over his father's business.

But the young man had different ideas. To the distress of his parents, he turned his back on the comfortable future they had prepared for him. He left home and dropped out of respectable society.

For a while he lived like a hermit in a lonely place, neglecting to eat while he struggled with the questions that haunt all sensitive young men: Who am I? What should I do with my life?

He emerged from this period of isolation with strong convictions he felt he must share with others. So he began to go from town to town, expounding his views on life to anyone who'd listen.

He had no money and lived like a vagrant, accepting such hospitality as was offered him. He often slept in the fields. Sometimes he went hun-

gry. But he refused to worry about where his next
meal was coming from; he thought there were more
important things demanding his attention.

He wasn't choosy about the company he kept.
Many of his friends were socially unacceptable and
some were notorious. One was a thief, another an
ex-prostitute.

His relatives were embarrassed by his behavior.
They pleaded with him to come home and go into
the family business. But he told them that wasn't
his bag.

Some people—mostly the poor, the sick and the
scorned—thought he was wonderful. He was clearly on their side. He even had the nerve to say they
were closer to God, in their misery and acknowl-
edged sin, than any of the self-righteous types who
made a big deal out of public performance of their
religious duties.

That kind of talk did not endear him to leaders
of the Establishment. Their annoyance with the re-
bellious young man escalated to outrage when he
began to challenge time-honored precepts of conventional morality.

He had this idea that loving other people—being
genuinely kind and compassionate toward *all* kinds
of people—was more important than keeping rules.
He contended no man could honestly say he loved
God if he hated or mistreated his neighbor.

What really upset the Establishment was his
claim that he was speaking not for himself but for
God. He could do so, he tried to explain, because
he was in constant close communion with God and
his one goal in life was to ascertain and do God's
will.

The powers decided he was either a lunatic or a

dangerous subversive. Either way, they figured, he had to be put down.

Perhaps if he'd been willing to cool it a bit they would have let him off with a few years in jail. But he was too committed to make compromises. He couldn't conform—not even to save his life.

So the Establishment framed him on a sedition charge, and he was executed like a common criminal.

You might think no good could possibly come from such a life. But you would be wrong. For that young man has had a greater influence for good than any other figure in human history.

His name was Jesus.

If you didn't recognize his life story, it's not surprising. Some of his alleged followers have been so intent on demanding acceptance of theological doctrines about him that they have almost succeeded in obscuring the human personality of this warm, outgoing, irresistibly lovable man of first-century Palestine.

This slighting of Jesus' humanity is done in the name of piety. But it isn't piety: it's heresy. The Church that calls him Lord insisted from its earliest days that, whatever else Jesus may have been, he was fully and authentically human.

If you want to get acquainted with God—to find out what He's like and what He expects of you—I know of no better way to begin than by getting acquainted with Jesus.

Forget, for the present at least, those baffling Christian doctrines about "incarnation" and "atonement." All you need know, in order to accept Jesus as your guide to God, is that he spoke about God with greater authority, simplicity and directness than any other person, before or since, has ever been able to do.

THE VISIBLE IMAGE OF AN INVISIBLE GOD

To Jesus, God was never simply a word or an abstract concept. He invariably spoke of God as a Reality directly perceived in his own inner experience. Others—many others—have confirmed man's capacity for a direct awareness of God. But in Jesus this God-consciousness seems to have been more continuous and more intimate than it has been for anyone else of whom we have knowledge.

Think of it like this: the divine spark—the spirit of God—is present to some degree in all of us. But most of us, most of the time, are so wrapped up in self, so preoccupied with expressing our own feelings and gratifying our own desires, that the presence of God is very hard for us or anyone else to detect in our lives.

But Jesus wasn't like that. He was an extraordinarily unselfish—and un-self-centered—person. He emptied himself of pride, vanity and ambition so that he could be completely open to God. A contemporary described him as "the visible image of the invisible God." Another way of putting it, perhaps more meaningful to a modern mind, is that we can see in the personality, the life style and the teaching of Jesus as much of the character of God as can be expressed within the limitations of a human life.

So if you want to know what God is like, take a close look at Jesus. "The heart of Christian doctrine," says Dr. Arthur Michael Ramsey, Archbishop of Canterbury, "is that God is Christlike."

To preserve authentic memory of Jesus and

transmit it from generation to generation, a community came into being. Originally, it was a very informal fellowship bound by mutual love and a common loyalty to Jesus. Eventually it grew into an institution with all the advantages of strength, size and continuity and all the disadvantages of rigidity, authoritarianism and self-concern that characterize institutions.

This institution is called the Church. Even though it now seems to bear little resemblance to the original Christian community, it must be credited with at least one great service, which is sufficient to justify its existence. With all of its shortcomings, and even through the darkest hours of its history, it has somehow managed to keep alive the memory of Jesus, the Man for Others, the Man Who Knew God.

HOW TO READ THE NEW TESTAMENT

Early in its history, the Church recognized the need to set down its memory of Jesus in writing while the eyewitness generation was still alive. The recognition of this need led to the collection of writings we call the New Testament.

Biblical scholars haggle endlessly over the proper interpretation of the New Testament record: how much may be regarded as a historically accurate account of actual events, and how much uses the language and imagery of myth to convey truth too inward to be reached by reporting external facts.

I see no reason why you should get involved in this controversy. All you really need to understand, before you begin reading the accounts for yourself, is this: most competent scholars now agree that the vivid impression of Jesus which emerges from these records is an authentic portrait of a real person. When you have finished reading them, I believe you will agree with the great English Bible translator J. B. Phillips: "No man could have invented such a character as Jesus."

The four New Testament gospels,* which are our main source of information about the life of Jesus, are not full-length biographies. They are more like magazine profiles. They give us a strikingly clear picture of Jesus through a succession of anecdotes about what he did and said and how he behaved in various circumstances. But they do not contain a great amount of connected narrative. And they omit many details which a modern biographer would include as a matter of course.

For example, none of the gospels gives a physical description of Jesus. We may infer that he was a tall man, because he was easily spotted in crowds; that he was muscular and sun-bronzed, because he lived a rugged outdoor life; and that he wore long hair and a beard because nearly all Jewish men did in his day. Aside from these logical inferences, the thousands of "portraits" of Jesus that have been painted over the centuries are based entirely on artistic imagination.

If you are carrying around in your mind a mental image of Jesus derived from some insipid picture you were shown in Sunday school long ago, and if this image turns you off, you may feel free to turn it off and construct your own portrait as you read the gospels. Chances are it will be a far more virile one—and closer to the truth.

I am assuming, you see, that you will read the New Testament. You must do so if you really want

---

*The word "gospel" is derived from an Anglo-Saxon phrase signifying "good news."

to learn about Jesus. But you don't have to read it all at one gulp. In fact, I would strongly recommend against starting at the beginning and going right through to the end. My advice is that you read first the Gospel According to Luke, a relatively brief work (about 20,000 words) that is one of the literary masterpieces of all time.

After finishing Luke, read The Acts of the Apostles, which is a sequel written by the same author. It gives the history of the early Church. Then you can go on to some of Apostle Paul's letters to young churches of Asia Minor, or go back to read another of the gospels. Don't try to read more than one or two chapters at a time. Digest them for a while before you go back for more.

Be sure to get a good modern translation. The old King James Version, which probably is lying around your house somewhere, is so archaic in its English that it is sure to baffle or mislead you. Invest in a paperback copy of *Good News for Modern Man*, the American Bible Society's wonderfully readable translation of the New Testament. Or spend a little more for the excellent *New English Bible* or *The Jerusalem Bible*.

In reading the gospels, it is important to bear in mind that Jesus made frequent use of hyperbole— obvious and intentional exaggeration—to shock his listeners out of well-worn mental ruts and open their minds to new insights. There is no greater insult to the memory of this great master of the art of communication than to take his flashing metaphors literally, as many people today unfortunately are inclined to do.

If the miracle stories bother you, as they probably will, remember there are many devoted Christians who don't take these stories literally. Read them as you do the parables of Jesus—to see what point the story is trying to make. Of course, if we're really open-minded about it, we must recognize that the "miraculous" events may really have occurred exactly as described. To deny their possibility is as arbitrary as insisting they *must* have happened. If Jesus was an open channel through which the love of God could flow, as the record clearly indicates he was, is it unreasonable to believe that some rather extraordinary things took place among the people who came into contact with him?

We know, in fact, that some extraordinary things did take place. A timid fisherman became a bold leader of men. A raging bigot became a gentle apostle of love. A madwoman became serene. A whore became a saint. Are these transformations of inner character any less "miraculous" than the healing of a physical infirmity? Obviously not. It is simply a case of our minds having been conditioned to accept psychological miracles and reject physical miracles.

Frankly, I don't think it matters greatly how you interpret most of the miracle stories in the gospel. But there is one which I feel must be taken seriously as a historical account of an event that really happened. And it is the most difficult of all for modern minds to find credible.

When Jesus was executed, his panic-stricken followers dispersed and fled in all directions to hide. In the normal course of human events, that would have been the end of the story. The world would never have heard of Jesus.

But a short time later we find his followers reassembled in Jerusalem, no longer timid and afraid, boldly proclaiming that Jesus had risen from the dead. This much is well-attested history.

The question is: did it really happen? Or was it just a myth invented by disciples who could not reconcile themselves to the loss of their beloved teacher?

Obviously, no one is able now to make dogmatic declarations about the reality or non-reality of an event alleged to have happened two thousand years ago.

What can be stated as abundantly documented historical fact is that there were witnesses—not two or three, or a dozen, but several hundred—who claimed to have seen and talked to Jesus after his death.

These witnesses were not hallucination-prone mystics. They were farmers, fishermen and housewives. They knew as well as you and I that dead men usually stay dead, and they were fully as surprised as we would be to encounter an exception to this universal rule of human experience.

The depth and sincerity of their conviction are attested by their readiness to lay down their lives for it. Many of them cheerfully accepted martyrdom rather than deny the reality of the incredible event they said they had witnessed.

Some modern scholars get around the difficulty of believing in a physical resurrection by suggesting that Jesus' return to life was a subjective experience which took place in the minds and hearts of his disciples. If you find this theory congenial, by all means embrace it. Certainly it makes more sense than some of the bizarre "explanations" that depict a deeply drugged Jesus returning to consciousness in the cool of a tomb. To accept *that* notion, you have to be able to believe that tough

Roman legionnaires were naive enough to hand over a condemned criminal to his friends without first making sure he was really dead.

Before you decide how you will interpret the story of the resurrection, I suggest you read all five versions of it (one in each gospel and a fifth in Paul's first letter to the Christians of Corinth). You will find they differ slightly in the details they give of Jesus' post-resurrection appearances. As a reporter, I find these minor discrepancies quite significant. Whenever you collect eyewitness accounts of any event, you find these little variations in detail. To a working newsman, they are the stamp of authenticity, whereas five fully harmonious accounts would strongly suggest that somebody had been tempering with the original reports to make them dovetail.

None of this constitutes proof, of course. What it comes down to is this: a person who believes that the resurrection *could* happen will find ample historical evidence to justify his believing that it *did* happen. But there can never be enough evidence to convince a person who has decided in advance that it could not possibly be true. It's a choice each of us must make for himself.

Personally, after doubting it for a very long time, I have finally come to the conclusion that it really happened. Two things have impelled me toward this view. First, I find it impossible to account for the birth of the Christian community unless something very extraordinary took place to embolden the frightened little band of Galileans who fled into hiding after Jesus was executed.

Second, and more important, the longer I think about the kind of person Jesus was and the kind of life he led, the more appropriate it seems to me that God should have honored <u>him</u> and vindicated <u>his teaching through an event of uniquely startling impact.</u>

If you find yourself unable at present to accept the possibility of physical resurrection, don't sweat and strain over it. If you're prepared to believe that the spirit of Jesus is still present in the world, and that the memory of Jesus still gives us our best clue to what God is like, that's quite enough to be going on with.

<u>Accepting Jesus as a guide to God, trying to em- ulate his life style, and obeying his commandment to love are infinitely more important than giving affirmation to theological dogmas about him.</u> He said so himself.

Dr. Albert Schweitzer, who gave up a brilliant career in Europe to go to tropical Africa and establish a hospital, was not an orthodox Christian and there were many dogmas of the Church that he was never able to accept. But he did accept Jesus, unreservedly, as the Lord of his life.

"Anyone who ventures to look the historical Jesus straight in the face and listen for what he may have to teach him in his powerful sayings, soon ceases to ask what this strange-seeming Jesus can still be to him," Schweitzer said. "The true relation to him is to be taken possession of by him."

6

The Hard Test

You don't have to take my word—or Albert Schweitzer's or St. Paul's—that Jesus is a reliable guide to God. You can put the claim to empirical test. Indeed, you must do so if Jesus is to be any real help to you.

You put Jesus to the test by actually living the way he taught men to live.

This is not easy to do. It doesn't come natural to anyone. It may require radical changes in your attitudes and customs. It will entail painful sacrifices of what you have hitherto regarded as your inalienable right to look out for your own legitimate self-interests. And it's all a gamble, from your point of view, for there's no way of being sure in advance that this rocky path leads somewhere worth getting to.

But if you're courageous enough (or desperate enough) to risk something on the proposition that Jesus may have the key to meaningful life, you'll find it's the best bet you ever made. At least, I did, and that's why I'm touting it so strongly to you.

If I knew of a short cut I'd tell you about it. But

it seems to be the common experience of all seekers in all ages that the only way to discover the validity of Jesus' approach to life is to try it.

THE TRULY RADICAL TEACHINGS

If you judge his teachings in the light of "common sense" or by any other rational standard, you'll reject them. They *don't* "make sense" in the world's terms. That is why they are so truly and profoundly radical: they literally turn upside down much of the conventional wisdom of the world.

Nor can you fairly judge Jesus' teachings on the assumption that their results can be seen in what is commonly but most inaccurately called "Christian civilization." As G. K. Chesterton pointed out, "Jesus' way has not been tried and found wanting; it has been found hard and not tried." Some of Jesus' insights and parts of his value system have subtly permeated our society, and are cherished today by many young rebels who would be surprised, and perhaps appalled, to learn that their radical ideas can be traced back to an itinerant rabbi who taught in Palestine two thousand years ago. But for the most part society in our time, as in his own, has successfully resisted subversion of its guiding principle of self-interest by the revolutionary ethic of Jesus.

The careless way in which the prefix "Christian" is attached to civilizations, nations and institutions is a measure of the degree to which the world has misunderstood, and continues to misunderstand, the plainest teachings of Jesus. The view is very widely held—among sharp critics as well as pious members of the Church—that "being a Christian" is primarily a matter of subscribing to certain beliefs about Jesus: that he was "the Son of God," that he "died for our sins," etc. But Jesus said explicitly on several occasions that he counted as his followers not those who gave him lip service but those who actually practiced his way of life.

"What is the point in calling me, 'Lord, Lord,' without doing what I tell you to do?" he asked his followers.

At his last supper with his closest companions, shortly before he was put to death, he emphasized again and again that obedience, not verbal piety, is the door which opens into authentic life.

He also was quite explicit about the reward a person can expect to receive for obediently following the way he taught. It is not wealth or "success" or protection from the pains and vicissitudes of life. It is the ineffable joy of entering *here and now* into a close, personal, conscious relationship with God.

COMMUNION WITH GOD

To Jesus, communion with God was the most desirable thing in the world, a thing so precious, so productive of happiness and fulfillment, that it is worth sacrificing everything else to attain.*

It is necessary to stress this fact, because anyone who seeks to use God as a means to some other end (such as security) will find the way of Jesus of little value in that endeavor. It is true that those who seek God for His own sake find their lives irradiated with numerous incidental blessings, including a deep peace and an abiding sense of liberation. But

---

*This is the point of many of Jesus' parables about "the Kingdom of Heaven." You will find the gospels much easier to understand if you remember that this often-used phrase, Kingdom of Heaven, may be taken as a synonym for communion with God.

if you put those things first, and seek God only as a means to them, you will find neither. That's what Jesus taught, and human experience has abundantly confirmed his warning.

✳ THE TWO GREATEST COMMANDMENTS

If you grasp that point—that God comes first or not at all—you already are well embarked on the way of Jesus. "You must love the Lord your God with all your heart, and with all your soul, and with all your mind," Jesus said. "This is the greatest and most important commandment."

"Love" is a verb of many meanings, and you may find yourself wondering how you can love God before you get to know Him well. If this question bothers you, feel free to substitute "seek" or "yearn after" or even "value" for "love." You can make any of those changes without losing the basic point of Jesus' teaching.

The second most important commandment, Jesus said, is, "You must love your neighbor as yourself." Again, it may be helpful to substitute other words for that much-abused and dangerously ambiguous verb "love." The sense of Jesus' teaching perhaps is best conveyed to a modern mind by reading it: "You must seek your neighbor's welfare, uphold his rights and defend his interests as zealously as your own." It is not required that you indulge in the hypocrisy of pretending to find your neighbor a likable and admirable fellow if in fact you regard him as a liar, a gossip, a blowhard or a nuisance. The point is that even if you find him execrable you must act toward him with as much kindness and good will as you would feel toward the person you love best.

That is a very hard rule to follow. And Jesus made it even more difficult by adding two further requirements. You <u>must continue to love your</u> neighbor—in the sense of <u>sincerely seeking his wel-</u> <u>fare</u>—even if he does you <u>grievous wrong and be-</u> <u>haves toward you with undisguised hostility.</u> That is the point of those oft-quoted but seldom-practiced admonitions from Jesus' "Sermon on the Mount" about loving your enemies and turning the other cheek.

The other difficult dimension which Jesus added to the commandment is found in his famous Parable of the Good Samaritan, which you'll find in Chapter 10 of Luke's gospel.* This vivid little anecdote is perhaps even more relevant to men living in the depersonalized urban society of our time than it was to the original audience in first-century Palestine. Its point is that <u>your neighbor, whom</u> <u>you are commanded to love, is anyone anywhere</u> <u>who needs help you are in a position to provide.</u>

Jesus said all other guide lines which human beings need to live good, useful and meaningful lives can be derived from these two great commandments. If you treasure your relationship with God <u>above all else, you will be as eager to comprehend</u> <u>and do His will as a child is to please a much-loved</u> <u>father. If you put your fellow man's rights and in-</u> <u>terests on a par with your own, you will welcome</u> <u>an opportunity to help him, directly or indirectly,</u> <u>and you will never treat him (or her, the pronoun</u> <u>having a particular relevance in this context) as a</u> <u>thing to be used for your own comfort, advance-</u> <u>ment or gratification.</u> That people—*all people*—are precious is not a newly discovered truth. It is the

*For convenient reference, the parable is reprinted in Appendix A.

sum and substance of the way that Jesus taught twenty centuries ago.

Although Jesus was not a legalist—he abhorred the very idea of a legalistic code that tries to spell out exactly what a man's duties are in every situation—he did suggest some practical inferences to be drawn from the basic law of love.

Be generous, he said, not only in sharing your possessions with those less fortunate, but also in your judgments of others. "Do not condemn others, and God will not condemn you," he said. "Forgive others, and God will forgive you. Give to others, and God will give to you. . . . The measure you use for others is the one God will use for you."

This promise that God will treat us as we treat our fellow man would be terrifying if it stood alone. But, like all of Jesus' statements, it must be read in the context of his total teaching. And that, fortunately, makes clear that God is in fact much more merciful to us than we are to each other. God is merciful because it is His nature to be so, not because we deserve leniency.

This knowledge is indeed comforting, but it should not lead anyone to complacency, for it too is qualified, in its turn, by Jesus' warning that presuming on God's mercy, by blithely taking it for granted, is the ultimate insult to His love and the one human attitude which He finds altogether intolerable. Thus, if we accept Jesus as our guide to the character of God, we will have a holy fear of divine wrath, born of the knowledge that we richly deserve chastisement. At the same time, we will have a serene confidence in God's readiness to forgive us at the first instant we show any sign of wanting a reconciliation with Him.

Does that sound paradoxical? Well, you may as

well get used to it. A great deal of Jesus' teaching is like that—holding two seemingly contradictory truths in tension, insisting that their relationship is both-and, not either-or. That is why simplistic readings of the gospel, which tear one statement out of its total context, can be so disastrously misleading.

THE TWO PERFECT SHORT STORIES

This particular paradox—that God both holds us strictly accountable for the way we treat others, and also is ever ready to forgive our lapses—is very close to the core of Jesus' message. It is a recurrent theme of his teaching, and is perhaps most vividly expressed in two of the gem-perfect short stories which he liked to tell when trying to explain profound truths.

One of these stories, recorded in the twenty-fifth chapter of Matthew's gospel, depicts the Day of Judgment when God separates the good men from the bad men. Not a question is asked, not a word said, about the performance of ritual religious duties. The one issue is how a man treated the poor, the hungry, the sick, the outcast and oppressed.*

The other story, which emphasizes God's eagerness to be reconciled with even the most wayward of His children, is the famous Parable of the Prodigal Son. It tells of an extravagant and undisciplined young man who demanded his freedom and was given it, along with a large sum of money to support himself.

He left home, took up with a wild crowd and quickly ran through his fortune in reckless spending. When his friends deserted him and hard times

*This story is reproduced in Appendix A.

came upon the land, he found himself lonely, hungry and despondent. He was ashamed to ask his father to take him back into the household as a son. But out of sheer need he resolved to ask for a job as a hired hand on his father's farm.

So he started home, doubtless dreading, as many other young men have done in similar circumstances, the "Well, I tried to warn you . . ." lecture which he had every right to expect as his greeting.

But the father in this parable represents God. And it is infinitely reassuring to all of us prodigals to hear from Jesus that the young man "was still a long way from home when his father saw him; his heart was filled with pity and he ran, threw his arms around his son, and kissed him."*

The moral of the story is quite clear: when you've done wrong, and know it, you don't have to go crawling back to God to plead for forgiveness. All you have to do is stop running away from Him long enough to let Him reach out and gather you safely into His arms.

And that holds true no matter who you are, or how far you've strayed, or what you've done.

---

*If you want to read the original, and I advise you to because Jesus was a much better storyteller than I am, you'll find the biblical passage (Luke 15:11—32) reproduced in Appendix A.

7

Encountering God

"Religion begins when God outwardly argued is inwardly experienced," said Harry Emerson Fosdick. "God outside of us is a theory: God inside of us becomes a fact."

Several times in the preceding chapters I have assured you, in what you may have regarded as an insufferably glib way, that you can attain firsthand knowledge of God by experiencing His presence in your own life.

It is now time to consider where and when and how this encounter with God takes place.

Where is the easiest question to answer. The place to find God is not in the stars, or in history—though He is present in both—but within your own heart. That is what Jesus meant when he said, "The realm of God is within you." It is what Martin Buber meant when he spoke of God as "the actual Other who meets me in my soul."

When also is a question quickly answered. The answer is: now. You don't have to wait for God to enter your life at some future time. The very fact that you are sufficiently interested in Him to be reading this book is adequate proof that He is already at work within you. For it is God who prompts us to seek Him. A hunger for God is always the first intimation of His presence. Once you grasp that basic fact, you can learn to recognize other signs of His activity in the depths of your being.

How God acts within us is a harder question, because it can be answered only by pointing to a mystifying but unmistakably real Presence or Power to which men have given a wide variety of names, including Spirit of God, Spirit of Christ, Spirit of Truth, Holy Spirit, Holy Ghost, Holy Comforter, Indwelling God and Inner Light.

For convenience, and because it is the reality rather than the name that matters, I shall refer to this Presence simply as the Spirit. Also, because the Spirit's relations with men are intensely personal, it seems more appropriate to use the personal pronoun, He, rather than the impersonal It. But I hope this capitulation to the tyranny of inadequate language will not mislead you into trying to conceive of the Spirit in anthropological images or impose any spatial or temporal limitations on His presence and activity.

For there are no such limitations. The first fact to be learned about the Spirit is that He cannot be imprisoned in institutions or manipulated by rites. The Church at times in its history has been tempted to forget this and to behave as though it could exercise some kind of monopoly control of the Spirit. But the Church's own source book, the New Testament, plainly states that the Spirit's activity is unfettered and unpredictable. It is orthodox Christian teaching—as well as observed fact—that the Spirit is constantly at work outside the

Church, in the hearts and minds of men who do not think of themselves as Christians in any sense, and who may not even believe in God.

Sometimes, and the present clearly seems to be such a time, the power of the Spirit as a motivating force for good is manifested more dramatically in movements and events that are not specifically religious than within the institutional life of the Church.

When all this is said, however, it remains true that the Spirit has a special relationship with the Church. For it was the Spirit who brought the Church into being and provided the enormous vitality which enabled it to grow in little more than a century from a tiny sect in Jerusalem to a fellowship extending throughout the Roman world.

THE POWER OF THE SPIRIT

The second chapter of the New Testament book of Acts gives a graphic account of the day (now celebrated in churches as "Pentecost") when the disciples of Jesus first felt themselves "filled with the power of the Spirit."

The disciples were huddled together in a house in Jerusalem. Jesus had ceased his postresurrection appearances to them some time before, and they didn't know where to turn or what to do. "Suddenly there was a noise from the sky which sounded like a strong wind blowing, and it filled the whole house where they were sitting. Then they saw what looked like tongues of fire spreading out; and each person there was touched by a tongue. They were all filled with the Holy Spirit and began to talk in other languages, as the Spirit enabled them to speak."

The Greek physician Luke who was the author of Acts was given to poetic imagery, and it would be a mistake to read this moving passage with that grim Teutonic literalmindedness that has afflicted so much scriptural interpretation. We don't need to reconstruct the exact physical details of the disciples' experience on Pentecost: it is sufficient to understand that something tremendous happened to them or, more precisely, *within* them.

That it radically changed all of them is abundantly evident from their subsequent actions. One moment they were hiding; the next moment they were in the streets of Jerusalem flinging the proclamation of their gospel into the teeth of the same authorities who had crucified Jesus. And a short time later they were carrying their message across seas, deserts and mountains, always risking and often losing their lives, caring nothing for danger, hardship or deprivation, fired with irresistible enthusiasm, and almost literally drunk with joy.

The disciples were well aware of the remarkable transformation that had taken place in their character and personality, and they were very emphatic in declining to take any credit for it themselves. They had become brave and generous and compassionate and self-sacrificing, not through any earnest striving after self-improvement, but solely because they had been massively infused with "the power of the Spirit."

During the twenty centuries that have lapsed since Pentecost, millions of others have experienced this "power of the Spirit" to heal infirmities of character, effect a basic alteration of disposition, and enable a person to behave with greater courage, compassion and unselfishness than he would ever be able to do by his own strength.

I, too, have experienced this Power-from-beyond-self. The imperfect but strikingly perceptible change it has wrought in my own essentially nasty disposition is one of the reasons I am so convinced of the reality of God. No amount of argument could persuade me that what I have experienced was the result of autosuggestion or any other "natural" working of the unconscious mind. But this explanation is bound to occur to you, and I know of no way in which anyone can prove that *any* experience he feels he had undergone was not merely a subjective phenomenon.

SCIENTISTS SPEAK

As a product of a contemporary culture that adulates science, you may find more persuasive the testimony of a distinguished scientist, the pioneer of modern psychology, William James. After long years of investigation, which are detailed in his classic text on *The Varieties of Religious Experience*, Professor James concluded that the widespread human experience of "union with the More" is not an illusion to be explained on psychological grounds, but a valid phenomenon in the realm of objective reality.

"The further limits of our being plunge into an altogether other dimension of existence from the sensible and merely 'understandable' world," James said. "Name it the mystical region, or the supernatural region, whichever you choose. . . .

"Our ideal impulses originate in this region. . . . When we commune with it, work is actually done upon our finite personality for we are turned into new men. That which produces effects within another reality must be termed a reality itself. God is the natural appellation of this supreme reality."

If you suspect James of being pre-Freudian and old hat, here is the view of Sir Frederick Bartlett, contemporary professor of psychology at Cambridge University:

"I cannot see how anybody who looks fairly at a reasonable sample of actions claiming a religious sanction can honestly refuse to admit that many of them could not occur, or at least that it is highly improbable that they would occur in the forms in which they do, if they were simply the terminal points of a psychological sequence, every item in which belonged to our own human, day-to-day world.

"It seems to me that genuinely religious people have done, effectively and consistently, many things which all ordinary sources of evidence seem to set outside the range of unassisted humanity. When they say 'It is God working through me,' I cannot see that I have either the right or the knowledge to reject their testimony."

I cite these scientific sources, not because I think they prove the reality of "the power of the Spirit," but simply to alert you to the fact that if you should choose to reject the claim that such a power exists you can't do so on "scientific grounds."

I am hoping, of course, that you won't reject it. Having learned what a difference it can make in your life when you touch this high-voltage line, I hate to see anybody else pass up the opportunity.

AT PEACE WITH OURSELVES

Enabling us to rise above ourselves is only one of the ways in which the Spirit effects a transformation of our lives. For God does not merely want us to be good. He also wants us to be happy and free and at peace with ourselves. We want these things, too, but most of us, unfortunately, spend most of our lives looking for them in the wrong places. St. Paul, in whom the Spirit wrought as remarkable a transformation as has ever taken place in any human being, included in one of his letters a lyrical listing of "the fruits of the Spirit"—the blessings which come pouring, unbidden and unexpected, into the life of a person who has fully opened his heart to the power of the Spirit.

The indwelling Spirit imparts, Paul said, "love, joy, peace, patience, kindness, goodness, faithfulness, gentleness, self-control." You may be sure that every item on that list was thoughtfully considered: it is a roster of the traits that Paul conspicuously lacked before he was, as he put it on another occasion, "taken possession of" by the Spirit.

The poet William Wordsworth was even more eloquent than Paul in his personal testimony to the impact of the Spirit:

> And I have felt
> A presence that disturbs me with the joy
> Of elevated thoughts; a sense sublime
> Of something far more deeply interfused,
> Whose dwelling is the light of setting suns,
> ... and in the mind of man.

A CHASTENING PRESENCE

Although the Spirit can and does bring a deep inner joy that cannot be erased by an external misfortune, He is not always gentle. He can also be a chastening presence.

"He can give us strength, but He can also show us our weakness," says J. B. Phillips, speaking out of a deep reservoir of personal experience. "He will show us more and more truth, but He also will shatter our illusions without scruple, especially illusions about ourselves. He will give us moments of wonderful perception, but will also allow us to endure terrifying darkness. He is indeed all goodness and light, but He will show no more compunction towards the evil things that we have allowed to grow in our hearts than a human surgeon would to a malignant growth."

Some people make the mistake of equating the Spirit with "the voice of conscience." But the two are not synonymous. The internal monitor we call our conscience may derive its standards from a vast variety of sources, including the mores of society, the expectations of our friends and the fear of getting into trouble. Quite often, the fact that our conscience doesn't "hurt" signifies not that an action was right but simply that our conscience is ill formed and flabby. Of course it is equally possible, and equally harmful, for a conscience to be neurotically overscrupulous. The role of the Spirit is not to take the place of conscience but to cleanse, instruct and guide conscience. This is one way in which the Spirit communicates with us—working within our conscience.

SPIRIT AND MIND

Another realm of the Spirit's activity, strongly emphasized in the New Testament but frequently overlooked today, is the intellect. Working through the natural processes of human thought, but at a level even deeper than intuition or the unconscious, the Spirit guides the minds of men in the search for truth.

And, it is important to bear in mind, this guidance is not restricted to those who consciously profess religious faith. Wherever men sincerely seek the truth, the Spirit is at work. A scientist who thinks of himself as an agnostic but is deeply dedicated to the pursuit of truth may be much more open to the guidance of the spirit than a religious fanatic with a closed mind.

THE SPIRIT AS WITNESS

Enabling, strengthening, uplifting, cleansing, guiding—we already have an impressive roster of the works of the Spirit. But His most important function has not yet been mentioned.

First and foremost, the New Testament teaches, the Spirit is a *witness* to the reality of God. It is the palpable presence of the Spirit that is our ultimate assurance of the three things we most need to know that God *is*, that God *cares* and that God is *accessible*.

As I have already indicated, we can *detect* the presence of the Spirit through the concrete results it has on our character, disposition and outlook.

But we also can sense the presence of the Spirit.

I have italicized that sentence because it may well be the most important statement in this book.

If you sincerely seek God, and persevere in the search for Him along the hard road of obedience, at some point in your quest, at a time and place and in a manner of God's own choosing, you will find yourself gripped by an unmistakable awareness of His presence. You won't ever be able to explain to anyone else—indeed, you may never fully comprehend yourself—exactly how you come to *know*, with absolute certitude, that you are in the presence of God.

The great Scottish theologian John Baillie has gone about as far as anyone can in making this experience rationally comprehensible. In his last book, *The Sense of the Presence of God*, published after his death in 1960, Professor Baillie noted that "the human spirit develops certain subtler senses or sensitivities which go beyond the bodily senses." He cited the familiar employment of such terms as a sense of beauty, a sense of humor, a sense of honor, a sense of propriety, a sense of proportion, a sense of duty.

"These are all refined or sublimate developments of our experience, and it is needless to say that they all presuppose for their possibility the experience gained through the bodily senses. Nevertheless, they carry us far beyond such experience, making us sensitive to aspects of reality of which the bodily senses, taken by themselves, could not conceivably inform us. They enable us to perceive something not otherwise perceptible; *to perceive* it, I say, and not merely to conceive it as a concept to which we are led by argument."

Baillie argued that every person has—or is capable of having—a "sense of the presence of God" which can be regarded as "a primary mode of apprehension." Like other basic human senses, it is *self-authenticating*. It requires no corroboration from other senses or from logical analysis: we simply sense that "we are in touch with reality."

The late Paul Tillich also believed that the sense of God has a self-authenticating quality about it. Tillich was never much interested in logical demonstrations of God's existence because, as he once said, he had an "immediate awareness" of God, so strong that argument was neither necessary nor possible.

Both Tillich and Baillie were preceded in this insight by a Hebrew poet who managed some three thousand years ago to express in a single rhapsodic sentence the conviction that God's presence can be directly sensed. Inviting everyone to share this rapturous experience, the author of the Thirty-fourth Psalm said: "O taste and see that the Lord is good!"

THE UNORTHODOX SEARCH

That the contemporary world is looking for just such an empirical approach to spiritual experience is evident, I think, in the tremendous upsurge of public interest in astrology, witchcraft, spiritualism and other "occult arts."

The people who are investing time and money in these superstitions, says psychotherapist Ludwig B. Lefebre, are seeking "ways to get beyond themselves" and establish "direct contact with a suprahuman agency."

It is a judgment on the so-called "main line" churches that this mass retrogression into ancient idolatries should take place in our supposedly enlightened age. "Direct contact with a suprahuman agency" is precisely what the Church was established to offer to men, and if people are having to look for it elsewhere, one can only conclude that the Church either has forgotten its primary mission or is doing a very poor job of letting the world know what business it's in.

This is a great irony, because the Church got into this plight as a result of its fervent efforts to prove itself "relevant" to man's everyday secular concerns. As part of this effort, many (not all) parts of the Church in recent years have gone to great ends to soft-pedal the supranatural, "other world" aspects of Christian teaching, and to present religion as a force for social betterment.

This approach was taken in the confident assumption that it would have far greater appeal to "modern man" than a lot of talk about such things as prayer, mystical experience and the "power of the Spirit"—the old-fashioned themes that were so prominent in the preaching of the early Church.

So now the Church finds "modern man" haring off after soothsayers, stargazers and necromancers of all types. In its obsession with relevance, the Church—or at least a large part of it—has made itself irrelevant.

THE PENTECOSTALISTS

Fortunately, not all of the Church has fallen into this pit. The Pentecostal denominations, once scorned as "holy rollers," have persisted in their fervent attachment to personal experience of the "power of the Spirit." I personally regret their tendency to become overly preoccupied with the phenomenon of ecstatic utterance (otherwise known as glossolalia or "speaking in tongues"). I would prefer them to remember that this was only one of many manifestations of the "power of the Spirit" mentioned in the records of the early Church, and that Paul felt it necessary to issue a public warning that too much attention to this one "charisma" was harmful because it was more likely to confuse or put off inquirers than to edify them.

But I also know that many Pentecostal leaders share my concern about this point, and are doing their best to balance such dramatic testimonies to the Spirit's presence with quieter and perhaps more meaningful ones, such as ministering to the poor and outcast (as, for example, the Assemblies of God are ministering, with astounding effectiveness, to youthful narcotics addicts in Harlem). So, in spite of my own inability, as a long-time, card-carrying Episcopalian, to enter fully into the joyous informality and spontaneity of Pentecostal worship, I greatly admire this movement and do not find it surprising that it is growing very rapidly at a time when many other churches are suffering declines in membership.

Other members of "main line" denominations have been impressed, as I am, by the Pentecostal emphasis on felt experience of the "power of the Spirit."

Within the past few years a substantial "charismatic movement" has developed among clergy and laity of the Episcopal, Roman Catholic, Lutheran, Presbyterian and Methodist churches. People are meeting in small groups, as the earliest Christians used to do, to pray together, study the Bible and share their deepest feelings and concerns. Many of these cells are to be found on college campuses—

not just in "Bible schools" but at places like Yale, Princeton, Chicago and Stanford.

Some of the participants in these "house church" meetings report they have experienced "speaking in tongues" and have found the phenomenon to be just as inexplicable and stirring as the New Testament indicates it was for the early church. "No one can adequately describe the experience," says the Rev. Charles L. Taylor, Jr., an Episcopal clergyman of the Washington, D.C., diocese. "Persons who have had it simply say it has changed their lives in a way that causes them to look at themselves and other people in a new light."

The Christian Church was created by "the power of the Spirit." Who knows? It may yet be revived, renewed and saved from its own folly by that same power.

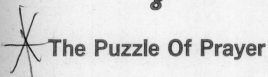

8

The Puzzle Of Prayer

Prayer is perhaps the most widely misunderstood of all human activities.

Many who profess to engage in it share with many who scorn it the mistaken idea that prayer is an Aladdin's lamp which men rub in the hope of inducing God to grant them special favors.

We can and should take our troubles to God in prayer. And we have the word of Jesus himself that it is perfectly proper to ask God for things—including very worldly and selfish things. But presenting petitions to God is not the only reason for praying: indeed, it is the least important of the many purposes of prayer.

Numerous attempts have been made to define prayer. But I've never come across a verbal formula that does full justice to all aspects of prayer. So, if you will bear with me, I shan't even try to give you a single definition. I shall merely sketch a rough map, delineating some of the things that prayer is and some things it is not, and offer a few practical suggestions about how you can make prayer a habitual and meaningful part of your life.

PETITION

We may as well begin with prayers of petition, for even though they are the least important kind, they also are the kind most familiar to most people. There are very few of us, I suspect, who do not instinctively resort to petitionary prayer in moments of great stress or anguish. It would take a rigorously consistent atheist to repress a silent cry of "God help me!" when his life was in dire jeopardy.

Although petitionary prayers well naturally from our hearts, our minds may have great difficulty in accepting their legitimacy. Logic tells us that if God is all-wise, He knows our needs without our telling Him about them, and if He is all-merciful, He will respond to those needs without being cajoled. Jesus made the point explicitly: "Your Father knows what things you need before you ask Him." Yet he taught his disciples to pray for such mundane necessities as daily bread. And, in his own prayers, he never hesitated to ask God's help in dealing with problems or averting tragedies.

The key to this apparent paradox can be found, I think, in the way Jesus began and ended his prayers. He began always by addressing God as "Father." Nothing is more basic to a close father-son relationship than an awareness on the part of the son that he can take *all* of his cares and troubles to his father and be sure of a sympathetic and attentive hearing. Asking God for help, even in the most transient and trivial of our concerns, is a way of affirming our filial dependence on Him.

A human father who really loves his son will not respond to all of his requests by automatically giving him exactly what he asks. Nor does a devoted

son expect such treatment. He credits his father
with wisdom as well as kindness, and he takes for
granted that there will be times when his father
must say no, either because the request is ill ad-
vised or because its denial will contribute to the
son's development into a mature and responsible
person.

The same recognition is implicit in the words
with which Jesus characteristically concluded his
prayers of petition, including his earnest plea in
the Garden of Gethsemane, a few hours before his
arrest, that God would spare him from the ordeal
of the cross. In that hour of deep human anguish,
Jesus prayed:

"Father, if it be Thy will, take this cup away
from me. *Yet not my will but Thine be done.*"

God did not remove the cup, and we can see now
why He couldn't. If Jesus had been spared the suffering and glory that awaited him on and beyond
the cross, he would have been just another itinerant rabbi who lived and taught to a ripe old age,
died a timely death, and was quickly forgotten.

There are passages in the New Testament which
seem to promise that God will grant any request
made of Him in prayer. These texts are cited by
people who look upon prayer as a kind of magic in-
cantation by which human beings may compel God
to give them what they want. But the passages obviously cannot mean any such thing, for the whole
New Testament record, particularly the account of
Jesus' prayer in Gethsemane, clearly refutes any
notion that God is honorbound to do everything we
ask of Him. He said no to the noblest petitioner
who ever lived, and it would be the height of arro-
gance for us to assume we have a stronger claim on
His benevolence than Jesus had.

Personally, I do not find it puzzling that God often declines to give us the specific favors we seek in petitionary prayer. What never ceases to amaze me is that petitionary prayers from very ordinary people for very ordinary things are sometimes granted, in a way that leaves no doubt in the mind of the recipient that God has heard and heeded his plea. I know this happens; it has happened many times to me, and I have seen it happen to others. I will not detail these events, because I realize that each of them can be explained away rationally as mere coincidence. Perhaps some of them were just that. But the cumulative effect of repeated experience has persuaded me, unassailably, that when people pray things happen that would not otherwise happen. Or as the late Archbishop of Canterbury, William Temple, put it: "When you stop praying, coincidences stop happening."

Anyone tempted to regard his "answered" prayers as a mark of special divine approbation will quickly be brought up short. The truth seems to be just the contrary. God is more apt to say no to a saint than to a neophyte in prayer, just as a human parent will be less indulgent toward a youth blossoming into manhood than a toddling child. The first thing to remember, when a petitionary prayer is granted, is that it is our weakness, not our goodness, that has appealed to God's mercy.

This may sound like a disincentive to spiritual growth. But people of long experience in prayer have not found it so. For when God denies an urgent request, He offers us something even better than the thing we asked. This alternative gift may be the strength to endure, and profit from, the ordeal we had asked Him to avert. Or it may be the

assurance that He loves us and is very near to us
even though He is allowing us to suffer. It is hard
to believe—there is no rational explanation for
it—but it is a fact attested by a great many people
that we are apt to be more certain of God's mercy,
more keenly aware of being ultimately secure in
His protecting arms, during the times of great ad-
versity, than in placid moments when all goes well
on the surface of our lives.

THE IMPORTANT DIALOGUE

We move with that observation toward a much
deeper dimension of prayer, one that is too rarely
explored in popular discussion of its efficacy. The
doorway to this new dimension is a clear recognition that prayer, when real, is never a monologue
in which we speak to (or at) God. It is a two-way
channel of communication, and the most important
messages that move over it are not those we transmit but those we receive.

An ancient sage wisely observed that, in prayer,
we should remember that "God gave us two ears
and only one mouth." It is good for us to talk to
God, to bring our cares before Him and seek His
help. But it is even better to *listen*.

I do not mean listen in the literal sense of ex-
pecting to hear a voice addressing us in English.
God communicates with us through His Spirit in
ways past understanding, and at a level of our
being far deeper than language can reach. The
nearest analogy I can think of is the radiotelemetry
through which vast quantities of precise data can
be transmitted instantaneously from a space satel-
lite to a ground-base computer, without ever being
translated into conventional verbal or mathemat-

ical symbols. When we say that God "speaks" to us
in prayer, we are simply using the best available
metaphor to denote a totally inexplicable phenomenon in which ideas, insights, aspirations, inten-
tions, hopes, desires and dispositions are implanted
in our minds and hearts by the Spirit of God who
dwells there.

We do not need to understand how it happens.
But we do need to learn how to "hear," or receive
and understand, these communications from God.
This is hard work that requires steady and disci-
plined effort. Even in our human relationships we
find it much easier to talk than to listen in the true
sense of opening ourselves to another person and
really caring what he has to say to us.

LEARNING TO LISTEN

The first step toward learning to listen to God is
to accept the fact that the universe exists to serve
His purposes, not ours. This may seem an elemen-
tal and obvious truth, but so great is our human
egocentricity that we are very likely to lose sight of
it. Only by reminding ourselves constantly that
God is the Creator, and we merely His creatures,
do we come to think of prayer as a way of bending
ourselves to God's will, rather than vice versa.

When we realize that prayer is first and foremost
an act of self-surrender, we understand why the
greatest of all prayers, which Jesus taught his disciples, begins with the words:

"Our Father in heaven,
"*Thy* name be hallowed;
"*Thy* kingdom come,
"*Thy* will be done . . ."

To say that prayer, slowly and attentively, while

associating ourselves wholly with its spirit of sub-
mission and obedience, is a good way to prepare for
listening for whatever God may have to say to us.

The next step is to cultivate the habit of holy silence. "No matter how God may choose to speak to
you," says Boston's great Episcopal preacher,
Theodore Parker Ferris, "you cannot listen until
you yourself are still. You must learn to sit still,
learn to be still, like the waters of a lake on a wind-
less day. This is perhaps one of the hardest things
in the world for a modern American to do, for we
have been brought up on the idea that there is
something sacred about activity, some inherent virtue in keeping busy."

Waiting in silent stillness is possible only in circumstances that assure you of at least a few minutes of uninterrupted solitude. That's why Jesus
often withdrew from human company—to a wilder-
ness, a mountaintop or an olive grove—when he
wanted to commune with God in prayer. And when
he couldn't get entirely away, he sought the privacy of a locked room or closet. In a modern home,
the temporary protection from outside distraction
which is essential to prayer is most likely to be
found in a bedroom or bathroom. The important
thing is to have a regular place for prayer in which
you can be reasonably sure no one is going to dis-
turb you, so that you are literally "alone with
God."

It helps to have a regular time as well as a cus-
tomary place for prayer. It doesn't particularly
matter when it is, so long as it is a time you can effectively safeguard from encroachment. Many people find early morning a good time for prayer. Others pray at the end of the day, just before retiring.
Choose the time that suits you best. But, having

chosen it, you should stick to it *every day*, including days when you are traveling or on vacation or in a hurry.

I am stressing the importance of a regular time and place for prayer in order to steer you away from the widespread but erroneous belief that prayer is genuine and helpful only when you "feel like" praying. Spontaneous prayers—the "flash prayers" that spring from our hearts at moments when we are particularly frightened or worried or relieved or grateful—are indeed precious, and you will miss my point entirely if you get the impression that I favor saving back all your praying for a particular time each day. What I wish to convey is that no matter how many "spot prayers" you offer in a day—and the more the better—you *also* need a set time to withdraw and compose yourself for communion with God, whether you happen to be in the mood for it or not. Only by keeping faithfully to a regular daily appointment with God can you make prayer what it ought to be—a deeply ingrained habit of turning toward God and consciously orienting yourself to His way.

There will be days—a good many, probably— when you find yourself unable to pray with any fervor or sincerity, or any sense of communion with God, no matter how hard you try. The greatest saints have told of going through such dry spells (one of them aptly described them as "the dark nights of the soul"), so it would be presumptuous of us garden-variety sinners to expect to avoid them.

When you are in such an arid period you will be tempted to feel that it is pointless or even hypocritical to go on praying. Don't believe it. The prayer appointments which you keep with God through a naked effort of will are perhaps even more valuable to your spiritual growth than those in which your heart and mind glow with confident faith and warm devotion. For in the dry periods your prayers are offered as a simple act of obedience. And it is through obedience, the deliberate and reiterated subordination of our desires to His will, that we must surely draw nigh to God.

I don't know of any way in which you can avoid occasional dry spells. But you can avoid boredom, which is an altogether different and far less useful condition. You will get bored with daily prayer if you allow it to settle into a monotonous routine, in which you keep covering the same ground over and over again.

Variety is the classic antidote for boredom. And it is quite easy to introduce variety into your prayers. A good method is to offer one type of prayer on Monday, another on Tuesday, still another on Wednesday, and so on, until you have made a complete rotation through the various possibilities.

THE FIVE KINDS OF PRAYER

Spiritual counselors have identified five major types of prayer, and if you want more variety than that you can divide some of them into subcategories.

The most common and familiar type is petitionary prayer, which we've already discussed. There is absolutely nothing wrong with it if it is offered in the spirit of Jesus—"not my will but Thine be done"—and if we make sure it doesn't become the only kind of prayer in which we engage.

Intercessory prayer might be called a special

form of petitionary prayer, but there are enough basic differences to warrant putting it into a class of its own. In petitionary prayer we ask things for ourselves (or for people, such as our children, in whose welfare we have a strong personal interest). In intercessory prayer we hold before God the problems and needs and hurts of other people. Intercessory prayer is a higher type than petitionary prayer, because it is born of compassion rather than self-concern. To be sincere, it must be accompanied by a genuine readiness to serve as God's instrument in relieving the need of the person for whom we pray. Jesus said we should engage in intercessory prayer not only for friends and persons who clearly deserve our sympathy but also for enemies and people who have behaved despicably. This is very, very hard to do but, when doggedly attempted, the effect on your attitudes and feelings can be quite remarkable. There is no surer way of learning to forgive someone who has wronged you or to love someone you've previously disliked.

The third type of prayer is called confession. In 3 it, we acknowledge our sins and accept God's forgiveness. It is an important type of prayer, not because groveling cries of remorse are necessary to appease God's wrath, but rather because our own awareness of wrongdoing erects a barrier of guilt between us and Him which can be overcome only by honest confession and repentance.

Repentance, it should be noted, does not mean conjuring up feelings of regret. It simply means "turning about"—recognizing that we've been on the wrong track and making a quiet decision to get on the right track. It is an act of will, not an emotion. The prayer of confession can be a joyous and liberating kind of prayer, if we bear in mind that

God is always more ready to forgive us than we are to admit we need forgiving.

4 Thanksgiving is the happiest kind of prayer. In it, we count our blessings and reflect on the kindness of the Father who caused or allowed these good things to happen to us. I think it important to be quite specific in giving thanks, not trying to run the whole gamut of our blessings in every prayer, but singling out a few things—big or little —that have made us glad or relieved or hopeful during the past day or so. You will enervate the whole proceeding if you try to list things you think you *ought* to be thankful for, instead of those which actually have aroused your gratitude. It is natural and right to be thankful for the restoration of health after you've been ill, for the safe homecoming of a child who has stayed out too late, for disasters that might have happened but didn't. And if you reflect for a while you'll think of many other blessings which are so constantly available you come to take them for granted—as, for example, the love and companionship of a good wife, or the loyalty of a faithful friend. It also seems right, to me at least, to thank God for the beauty He has scattered so profligately throughout the natural world—for the first warm morning of spring after a hard winter, the fragile wonder of a wild flower, the musical gurgling and splashing of a rushing stream.

But what if your spirits are brought low by anxiety or suffering, so that you are unable to respond in gladness to such things? Then thank God that He is there, and that no evil deed of yourself or another, no trouble, no sorrow, no loss, can ever separate you from His love.

5 Closely related to thanksgiving, but still higher in the hierarchy of devotion, is the prayer of praise

and adoration. In it, we say, in whatever words we find congenial, "I love You, God, not for what You've done for me, but simply for what You are." The Psalms of the Bible are a rich trove of prayers of praise and adoration. After three thousand years we can still sense, and share, the exultant love of the Hebrew poet who cried, "Bless the Lord, O my soul, and all that is within me, bless His holy name!" Other great hymns of praise can be found in the ancient liturgies of the Church: the *Te Deum*, for example, or the *Gloria in Excelsis Deo*.

HOW DO YOU PRAY?

Never hesitate to borrow, and make your own, prayers which have been composed by someone else. Far from stifling spontaneity, the use of pre-packaged prayers will help to make your own prayers more meaningful and varied, by directing your attention to topics of prayer that had not previously occurred to you. There are hundreds of "prayer books" on the market. Some are good, others rather poor. In Appendix B you'll find a list of some that I particularly admire and recommend as starter-fuel.

A few more points may be worth mentioning.

Be *natural* in your prayers. Speak to God in your own plain language, not in some stilted, artificial jargon of piety. After all, it's not your words that matter but the disposition of your heart. If it is turned toward God in prayer, it doesn't matter what words you use—or indeed, whether you use any words at all. Silent communion is close to the pinnacle of prayer.

Pray as long as you need or want to, and no longer. Jesus warned that long-windedness is not a virtue in prayer, and the model prayer he gave his disciples has only sixty-seven words. You should allow ample time for your prayers, so that you are not distracted by feeling hurried, and so you can attain the state of stillness requisite to listening. But it is not necessary that you filibuster through all the time you've allotted for prayer. Until you are very far advanced in spiritual life, you probably will find it difficult to sustain a prayerful mood (either speaking or listening) for longer than ten minutes. And it may take a lot of practice to work up to that.

The posture you assume in prayer does not matter to God but may make a difference to you. You can stand, sit, kneel or lie down to pray. Kneeling is a physical act of humility which helps some people prepare psychologically for prayer. An uncomfortable position may be a distraction, but one that is too comfortable—for example, lying in bed—is likely to lead to drowsiness rather than concentration.

Finally, remember that the greatest gift God can give you is Himself. Whatever else you ask, include in *every* prayer a request that the Spirit will so guide your mind and rule your heart that you will be able to want the things you ought to want, for only through the prompting of God can you reach the point of desiring above all else a sense of His presence.

9

Reflective Reading
Or Meditation

To summarize briefly what has been said in preceding chapters:

If we let Him, God makes Himself known to us, communicates with us, guides, strengthens, empowers and comforts us, through the presence of His Spirit in the depths of our own being. This communion takes place pre-eminently in prayer.

But not exclusively in prayer. We are now ready to consider some of the other ways in which God reveals Himself and His purposes to those who earnestly seek knowledge of Him.

Second only to prayer as a channel of divine-human communication is the practice known as meditation. If that ancient term intimidates you, think of it simply as *reflective reading*.

Reflective reading is quite different from ordinary reading. It is not meant to inform or entertain. Its purpose, in the words of the great Catholic scholar Friedrich von Hügel, is "to feed the heart and fortify the will by putting them in contact with God."

As is the case with prayer, reflective reading, to

be a significant factor in your life, must become a daily habit, not an emergency measure resorted to in moments of particular stress. I recommend that you set aside from ten to fifteen minutes each day for this kind of reading. Don't try to do it for more than a quarter of an hour at a stretch: that's about as long as anyone can sustain the mood of *open, receptive thoughtfulness* which distinguishes this from ordinary reading.

There is still another parallel with prayer. Reflective reading requires absolute privacy. Therefore you must find a time and place that will secure you, for this brief period, from interruption by telephone calls, family conversation or other distractions. My personal solution to this problem is to withdraw to a bathroom, lock the door and turn on the water taps in the wash basin. You will have to devise your own stratagem for achieving a brief solitude—which seems to be the one thing that modern life is bent upon denying us.

Remember that reflective reading is not meant to be a substitute for prayer. It's something you do *in addition* to your daily prayers. Some people prefer to put the reading period immediately prior to the prayer period. Others find it more helpful to separate the two: for example, by praying at the start of the day and reading in the evening. You might try both ways and see which suits you better.

Personal preference also must be the final arbiter in your choice of reading material. However, I can offer a few general guidelines and some specific suggestions that you may wish to try.

THE BIBLE

The basic idea is to find books that will focus your thoughts on God and your relationship with Him. The Bible is an excellent choice—provided you stick to those portions of it that are suited to this kind of reading. I would include all of the New Testament in that category, along with such Old Testament books as Psalms, Proverbs, Job, Isaiah, Amos, Hosea, Micah and—if you are fortunate enough to own a Bible that includes the Apocrypha —the great book of Hebrew wisdom known as Ecclesiasticus (*not* Ecclesiastes) or Sirach.

A good modern translation is not only desirable, it is absolutely essential if you wish to derive insight rather than confusion from Scripture reading. There are at least six superb English translations from which you can choose. My own favorites are *The New English Bible* and the American Bible Society translation known as *Today's English Version.* But I would also give high marks, for readability, clarity and beauty of language, to *The Jerusalem Bible*, the *Revised Standard Version*, the J. B. Phillips translation and the *New American Bible.* If you don't possess at least one of these translations, you simply have no idea how lucid, how strikingly relevant to today's concerns, the Bible can be.

Start with the Gospel According to Luke, which is, for my money, the most beautifully written book of the Bible and one of the masterpieces of world literature. I find it best to read no more than one chapter a day. If your Bible has modern typography, with subheads and paragraphs instead of the archaic chapter-and-verse structure which medieval printers imposed on the original biblical texts, you may choose to read only that portion, long or short, which is contained under one sub-heading. Most of the modern translations are very good about thus presenting the biblical material in coherent units rather than arbitrary "chapters."

After Luke, turn back to the Old Testament and work your way through the Psalms, that magnificent collection of ancient Hebrew poetry that Germany's martyr-theologian, Dietrich Bonhoeffer, called "the prayer-book of the Bible." There is a Psalm to speak to every human condition, from bleak despondency to rapturous joy.

After you've spent a few weeks among the Psalms, return to the New Testament and read the Gospel According to John. It is the most "theological" of the four gospels, and the only one which tries to express the Christian experience in the thought forms of classic Greek philosophy. Then move on to some of St. Paul's letters to the infant churches of Asia Minor, beginning with his two "epistles" to the Corinthians, and his *magnum opus*, the letter to the Romans.

I'm personally very fond of some of the so-called minor epistles of the New Testament, particularly those attributed to James and John. James is pithy and practical; John is a sublime presentation of the meaning and importance of love.

Although critical study of the Bible should have a place in your *ordinary* reading, it has no place in your reflective reading. If you come to a passage that baffles or repels you, or arouses skepticism, let it pass gently by. *Don't* get bogged down wondering whether a particular episode is actual history or a picture story meant to convey a moral. Your only question, during reflective reading, should be: *What relevance does this passage have for me, here* _and now?_ If you read the Bible in that spirit, you will be amazed how frequently God will be able to use its words to communicate with you about your most personal and immediate concerns.

But don't strain after messages. The worst thing you can do in Bible reading is to try to extort some personal application from every text. If the shoe doesn't slip right on, wait for a better fit. There will be many days when your period of reflective reading seems to yield nothing whatever that applies to you. Do not be disturbed about this. If you persist in the daily habit of reflective reading, you will receive ample sustenance over the long haul. Many passages which mean nothing to you when you first read them will pop out of your memory, much later, to shed light on some new situation or experience.

Although the Bible is the richest lode you can mine, it's by no means the only book that can serve as a vehicle for divine-human communication in reflective reading.

OTHER BOOKS

Any list of books suitable for this kind of reading is bound to be highly subjective. All I can do is mention a few that have meant a great deal to me, and invite you to browse among them until you have located the ones that are on your wave length. Incidentally, you don't need a huge larder of books for soul-feeding. A few favorites, returned to again and again, can last you a lifetime. The second or third or fourth reading of a passage often yields fresh and deeper insights than you ever found there before.

Next to the Bible in my own affections is _A_

Diary of Readings, which contains 365 one-page readings compiled by Scottish theologian John Baillie from many periods and traditions. It was published in 1955 by Charles Scribner's Sons and is still in print. Any bookstore can order one for you.

Next on my list is *George Macdonald, an Anthology*, edited by C. S. Lewis. Macdonald also was a Scot—perhaps the Scots have a special knack for this kind of thing. I agree completely with what C. S. Lewis says in his introduction: "I know hardly any other writer who seems to be closer, or more continually close, to the Spirit of Christ Himself than George Macdonald." You can make his acquaintance in a Dolphin paperback published by Doubleday & Co., Inc.

Another favorite of mine is *The Meaning of Being a Christian*, by Harry Emerson Fosdick. Like Baillie's book, it contains 365 daily meditations, one for each day of a year. This is not a compilation of the writings of others but is drawn entirely from Dr. Fosdick's own lucid and profoundly Christian books. It is published by Association Press.

Finally, I commend to you a little book that has been cherished by hundreds of thousands of people since it was first published in 1884: *Daily Strength for Daily Needs*, by Mary W. Tileston. This also contains a page of food-for-thought for each day of the year. I've been through it five times and am still learning from it. The publisher is Grosset & Dunlap, and you can find a copy in any good religious bookstore.

I have deliberately omitted from this very personal selection the great classics of devotional literature, such as the *Confessions* of St. Augustine,

The Imitation of Christ, by Thomas à Kempis, *A Testament of Devotion* by Thomas Kelly, and *Spiritual Perfection* by François Fénelon. These are all great books for reflective reading, and I omitted them from my list only because they are so well known that it seems unnecessary to call them to your attention.

THE THREE R'S

After you have chosen a time, a place and a book, you can begin to practice what someone has called the "Three R's" of meditation.

The first R, of course, is the actual *reading* itself.

The second R is *reflection*. Whenever you come to a sentence or phrase that seems to have something to say to you, stop reading and start thinking. Examine your problems attitudes, ambitions or desires in the light of the passage you've just read. Remember, you're not trying to justify yourself or lecture yourself: your sole purpose is to open your mind and heart to any guidance God may be trying to give you at this moment, through this passage. Upon due reflection, you may decide there wasn't actually a message there for you. Unless you reach that conclusion at least some of the time, you can be sure you're straining too hard.

The third R is *response*. When your reading leads to a fresh insight or conviction, respond to it in some immediate and practical way. What change can you make in *today's* plans or in an existing relationship, to bring your actions into line with the truth that you have just glimpsed? It is this "third R" stage that distinguishes meditation from mere musing. Genuine meditation should always lead to a concrete response.

10

God In Community

Prayer and meditation, as I have described them, are essentially *private* relationships with God. But God also addresses men and makes Himself known to them in *community*. One way in which you can encounter the reality of God, therefore, is by sharing in a *corporate experience* of His presence.

Meeting God in, through and with others is just as valid and meaningful as discovering His presence in the solitude of your own heart. Jesus bears witness to that. No one ever had a closer private relationship with God than he did. Yet no other religious teacher has ever laid such heavy emphasis on the importance of human fellowship as a way of drawing nigh to God.

The first act of Jesus' ministry was to create a community. He chose twelve men—none of them previously distinguished for sanctity—to travel with him as he went about Galilee teaching, healing and comforting the oppressed. These twelve "disciples" were his inner circle of constant companions. The gospels indicate there also were about sixty others, including several devout women, who were closely related to this first Christian community.

At the end of his ministry, as he shared a last supper with his disciples, Jesus urged them to remain together. "A new commandment I give you," he said. "Love one another. As I have loved you, so you must love one another."

The disciples did stick together. The New Testament records that on the day of Pentecost, when God poured forth His Spirit on the disciples and set their lives on fire with courage and purpose, "all the believers were gathered together in one place."

THE EARLY COMMUNES

During the first two centuries of its existence, when it radiated a vitality never since equaled, the Church was a highly informal association of local communes, in which believers shared their worldly goods with one another and drew courage and strength from each other to face common tasks and common dangers.

St. Paul's "epistles," which constitute a large portion of the New Testament, were simply pastoral messages to these isolated little communities of Christians. Not surprisingly, we find them a good deal of instruction in the ground rules of community life.

The basic principle, Paul said, is mutual dependence. Man is by nature a social being: his highest potential can be realized only in relationship with other human beings.

To stress the intimacy of our interdependence, Paul used a striking metaphor. All of us, he said, are members of one body. We are as necessary to each other as the foot, the hand, the eye and the ear. "There is no division in the body, but all its different parts have the same concern for one another," he noted. "If one part of the body suffers, all the other parts suffer with it."

Paul went on to spell out practical ways in which we can acknowledge our involvement with and responsibility for one another:

"No more lying. . . . Everyone must tell the truth to his brother, for we are all members together in one body. . . .

"Do not use harmful words in talking. Use only helpful words, the kind that build up. . . .

"Get rid of all bitterness, passion and anger. No more shouting or insults! No more hateful feelings of any sort! Instead, be kind and tender-hearted to one another, and forgive one another. . . .

"Help carry one another's burdens, and in this way you will obey the law of Christ."

COMMUNES OF TODAY

The Church is meant to be today what it was in the time of St. Paul—a community in which people love, understand, accept and support one another. Bigness, institutional self-concern and plain human weakness all too often keep it from bearing much resemblance to the loving fellowship envisioned by Jesus and Paul.

But despite its shortcomings the Church continues to be drawn toward and conditioned by its unrealized ideal. And that's why you can find today, both within and just outside the formal framework of the institutional Church, little groups of believers who are taking seriously the challenge of Christian living and working out its meaning together. These small but intimate fellowships are known by a variety of names: underground churches, house churches, ad hoc churches, prayer cells, encounter groups, study groups, discussion groups, etc. Not all of them are explicitly Christian. The fellowship of Alcoholics Anonymous, for example, is committed to no specific theological creed, yet I know of no place in which men and women in one particular kind of trouble are more certain of encountering a vital faith in the reality of God and the kind of mutually supportive human relationships which Paul described as the hallmark of Christian community.

I urge you to seek out some such group—attached to or apart from a regular church—in which you can share with others the insights and puzzlements, the joys and trials, the exultant moments of faith and the dark hours of doubt, the gnawing temptations and the sudden accessions of unexpected strength, that are a part of the great adventure of growing in the knowledge of God.

A close and continuing association with other pilgrims is the best and perhaps only effective safeguard against an excessive subjectivity which could cause you to mistake the projections of an overactive imagination for promptings from God, or, conversely, to ascribe to autosuggestion what was in fact a real communication of the Spirit. Having people to whom you can talk, openly and without embarrassment, about your religious experiences therefore serves both a corrective and a corroborative function.

But there is a still better reason for associating yourself with a group of people who are honestly trying to relate to each other in a Christian (i.e., loving) way. In the actual experience of loving another person, or being loved by another, you encounter God. Where love is, God is.

REVELATION THROUGH EVENTS

We also encounter God in *events*. This is the real meaning of the miracle stories of the Bible, which so many people today find puzzling or inconceivable. God reveals Himself to us, and makes known His purposes, through things that happen to us or around us.

I see very little to be gained from embarking on a long discussion of whether these revelatory events result from direct divine intervention in the ordinary processes of nature, or whether God simply utilizes things that happen as a result of the normal operation of natural cause and effect. Personally, I do not regard nature as a closed system, and have no difficulty accepting the possibility that the Creator of the system may see fit occasionally to introduce new elements of causation that lead to extraordinary effects. If God's will brought the universe into being, should that will not exert upon any component part of the universe, when He chooses, an influence as direct, potent and "natural" as gravity and magnetism?

That, however, is merely my own attitude, and I'm not going to try to cram it down your throat. I've learned that vast numbers of people today, while perfectly willing to believe that God acts *spiritually* in the world, simply cannot conceive of divine activity having *physical* results. I promise not even to point out the logical inconsistency of this popular attitude, or draw attention to the fact that it is no less "miraculous" or more "natural" for God to influence the thought patterns of a human brain than it would be for Him to restore the vitality of a heart or liver or kidney in a medically inexplicable healing.

I'm not going to argue these points because, for our present purpose, it matters not at all whether you choose to think of God as influencing the course of events or of influencing you to see those events in a particular light. The only thing I ask of you is that you be on the alert for any communications God may direct to you through happenings.

I know a woman whose whole outlook on life was changed because of an event that anyone else might have dismissed as trivial and insignificant. She was bowed down with a great load of anxiety, because of family problems, and had gone to her church to pray. Her prayers brought her no comfort, and she left the church full of doubt and despair. As she walked down the church steps she saw on the sidewalk a coin which evidently had dropped from the pocket of a passer-by. She stooped to pick it up and her eye happened to light upon the inscription: "In God We Trust."

"I suppose it sounds childish and silly," she told a friend years later. "But I knew, when I picked up that nickel, that I had received my answer. All I had to do was trust in God. And I've done so, from that day to this."

Did that woman experience a "miracle"? I would say yes, because in my opinion a "miracle" is any event, mundane or extraordinary, which God uses as a sign or signal to communicate with a receptive human being. Whether God deliberately arranges the event, or simply takes advantage of a pure coincidence, is something we can never tell and do not really need to know.

THE EVER-PRESENT COMFORT

It is not only in single events but also, and probably more often, through the general circumstances of our lives that God seeks opportunities to reveal Himself to us. I feel sure God tries to speak to us through our happiness and successes, but He often finds us inattentive then. We are most open to God when we are least confident of ourselves. Anxiety, suffering, hardship, defeat or bereavement can make us more keenly conscious of God's presence, and more certain of His love, than we're ever apt to be on the sunny days when all seems well with our world.

This is the ultimate answer to the "problem of evil." It's not an intellectual but an existential answer. Whatever human logic may say about the kind of world a loving God *ought* to have created, we all know from experience that it is in fact a hard, mystifying, often cruel world in which the best and kindest of men can get badly hurt. Some of us are lucky enough to have learned, also from experience, that God is present even—in fact, especially—in our pains and sorrows, and the sense of His presence is more than adequate compensation for *anything* we are called upon to endure.

This assurance—that God is with us and for us, and that nothing else really matters—is particularly applicable to the final human ordeal of death.

I do not profess to know exactly what awaits us beyond the exit portal of this life. How all this will be accomplished, I haven't the slightest idea. Nor do I greatly care. For, thanks to His abundant and persistent grace, I am now able to say with St. Paul:

"I am certain that nothing can separate us from His love: neither death nor life; neither angels nor other heavenly rulers or powers; neither the present nor the future; neither the world above nor the world below: there is nothing in all creation that will ever be able to separate us from the love of God."

Appendix A

Three Parables of Jesus

Here are the full texts of the three parables which were referred to in Chapter VI. To enable you to compare the styles of different biblical translations mentioned in Chapter IX, each of these excerpts is taken from a different version.

THE PARABLE OF THE GOOD SAMARITAN

And behold, a lawyer stood up to put him to the test, saying, "Teacher, what shall I do to inherit eternal life?" He said to him, "What is written in the law? How do you read?" And he answered, "You shall love the Lord your God with all your heart, and with all your soul, and with all your strength, and with all your mind; and your neighbor as yourself." And he said to him, "You have answered right; do this, and you will live."

But he, desiring to justify himself, said to Jesus, "And who is my neighbor?" Jesus replied, "A man was going down from Jerusalem to Jericho, and he fell among robbers, who stripped him and beat him, and departed, leaving him half dead. Now by chance a priest was going down that road; and when he saw him he passed by on the other side. So likewise a Levite, when he came to the place and saw him, passed by on the other side. But a Samaritan, as he journeyed, came to where he was; and when he saw him, he had compassion, and went to him and bound up his wounds, pouring on oil and wine; then he set him on his own beast and brought him to an inn, and took care of him. And the next day he took out two denarii and gave them to the innkeeper, saying, 'Take care of him; and whatever more you spend, I will repay you when I come back.' Which of these three, do you think, proved neighbor to the man who fell among the robbers?" He said, "The one who showed mercy on him." And Jesus said to him, "Go and do likewise."

Luke 10:25-37, *Revised Standard Version*

THE PARABLE OF THE LAST JUDGMENT

'When the son of Man comes in his glory and all the angels with him, he will sit in state on his throne, with all the nations gathered before him. He will separate men into two groups, as a shepherd separates the sheep from the goats, and he will place the sheep on his right hand and the goats on his left. Then the king will say to those on his right hand, "You have my Father's blessing; come, enter and possess the kingdom that has been ready for you since the world was made. For when I was hungry, you gave me food; when thirsty, you gave me drink; when I was a stranger you took me into your home, when naked you clothed me; when I was ill you came to my help, when in prison you visited me." Then the righteous will reply, "Lord, when was it that we saw you hungry and fed you, or thirsty and gave you drink, a stranger and took you home, or naked and clothed you? When did we see you ill or in prison, and come to visit you?" And the king will answer, "I tell you this: anything you did for one of my brothers here, however humble, you did for me." Then he will say to those on his left hand, "The curse is upon you; go from my sight to the eternal fire that is ready for the devil and his angels. For when I was hungry you gave me nothing to eat, when thirsty nothing to drink; when I was a stranger you gave me no home, when naked you did not clothe me; when I was ill and in prison you did not come to my help." And they too will reply, "Lord, when was it that we saw you hungry or thirsty or a stranger or naked or ill or in prison, and did nothing for you?" And he will answer, "I tell you this: anything you did not do for one of these, however humble, you did not do for me." And they will go away to eternal punishment, but the righteous will enter eternal life.'

Matthew 25:31-46, *New English Bible*

THE PARABLE OF THE PRODIGAL SON

(*The Lost Son*)

Jesus went on to say: "There was a man who had two sons. The younger one said to his father, 'Father, give me now my share of the property.' So the father divided the property between his two sons. After a few days the younger son sold his part of the property and left home with the money. He went to a country far away, where he wasted his money in reckless living. He spent everything he had. Then a severe famine spread over that country, and he was left without a thing. So he came to work for one of the citizens of that country, who sent him out to his farm to take care of the pigs. He wished he could fill himself with the bean pods the pigs ate, but no one gave him any. At last he came to his senses and said: 'All my father's hired workers have more than they can eat, and here I am, about to starve! I will get up and go to my father and say, "Father, I have sinned against God and against you. I am no longer fit to be called your son; treat me as one of your hired workers."' So he got up and started back to his father.

"He was still a long way from home when his father saw him; his heart was filled with pity and he ran, threw his arms around his son, and kissed him. 'Father,' the son said, 'I have sinned against God and against you. I am no longer fit to be called your son.' But the father called his servants: 'Hurry!' he said. 'Bring the best robe and put it on him. Put a ring on his finger and shoes on his feet. Then go get the prize calf and kill it, and let us celebrate with a feast! For this son of mine was dead, but now he is alive; he was lost, but now he has been found.' And so the feasting began.

"The older son, in the meantime, was out in the field. On his way back, when he came close to the house, he heard the music and dancing. He called one of the servants and asked him, 'What's going on?' 'Your brother came back home,' the servant answered, 'and your father killed the prize calf, because he got him back safe and sound.' The older brother was so angry that he would not go into the house; so his father came out and begged him to come in. 'Look,' he answered back to his father, 'all these years I have worked like a slave for you, and not once did I disobey an order of yours. What have you given me? Not even a goat for me to have a feast with my friends! But this son of yours wasted all your property on prostitutes, and when he comes back home you kill the prize calf for him!' 'My son,' the father answered, 'you are always at home and everything I have is yours. But we had to have a feast and be happy, for your brother was dead, but now he is alive; he was lost, but now he has been found.'"

Luke 15:11-32, *Today's English Version*

Appendix B

Prayer Books

Choosing a book of prayers is a highly personal matter. The ones I like best may not appeal to you at all. The important thing is to find one or more collections of prayers which seem to speak your language—not necessarily in the sense of saying things the *way* you normally do, but rather in the sense of expressing thoughts and aspirations and feelings with which you can identify. The whole value of a prepackaged prayer lies in reading it very slowly and thoughtfully and consciously making it *your* prayer.

As suggested earlier, the Book of Psalms in the Bible is full of great prayers, which have proved timely and relevant to men and women of many different cultures and backgrounds for three thousand years. The Psalms remain the prayer book *par excellence*.

I may be displaying my own bias as an Anglican, but I would give second place to *The Book of Common Prayer*, which has been cherished by millions for more than four hundred years, and which is the basis of worship in the Church of England, the

Episcopal Church and their sister churches of the world-wide Anglican Communion. Much of this ancient book is not directly relevant to private prayer, but you will quickly discover, in perusing it, how to find the magnificent prayers and "collects" which are scattered all through it. They are, in my estimation, the noblest creations of English prose outside of the now obsolete but ever beloved King James Version of the Bible. Like the King James, they may sometimes baffle you by using English words that have undergone a change of meaning since the Elizabethan age. But I've found that the sense of nearly all the prayers comes through quite clearly to a modern reader.

Among the many contemporary collections of prayers, here are some I particularly commend to your attention:

A Diary of Private Prayer by John Baillie, Scribner's, New York.

Book of Prayer for Everyman by Theodore Parker Ferris, Seabury Press, Greenwich, Connecticut.

Treasured Volume of Prayers, an anthology collected by John Scott, C. R. Gibson Co., Norwalk, Connecticut.

Prayers New and Old, Forward Movement Publications, 412 Sycamore St., Cincinnati 2, Ohio.

Nearly every major denomination publishes periodical devotional guides which contain daily prayers. If you attend a church, look at its tract rack, or ask the pastor, for a copy of the current edition. The quality of these booklets varies enormously, and you'll just have to shop and sample for yourself.

Appendix C

Other Books Recommended for
Additional Reading

For your convenience, I've grouped books according to the *needs* which, in my judgment, they are most likely to meet. Many of them are sufficiently broad in scope to be listed under several headings, but that would lengthen and complicate the listing, so I've arbitrarily assigned each book to what seemed to me its most appropriate category.

Within each category, books are listed more or less in order of ascending complexity—the easiest to read come first, the more difficult ones later. None of the books recommended, however, is beyond the comprehension of any intelligent layman who's willing to invest a little mental sweat in widening the horizons of his thoughts about God and man.

BOOKS TO READ WHEN YOU'RE TROUBLED BY THE
THOUGHT THAT IT REALLY ISN'T QUITE INTELLECTU-
ALLY RESPECTABLE TO BELIEVE IN GOD

Nature and God by L. Charles Birch, Westminster Press, Philadelphia. This inexpensive paperback, written by a distinguished biologist, is a masterful presentation of contemporary theology in a form congenial to a science-oriented mind.

A Rumor of Angels by Peter L. Berger, Doubleday, New York. A noted social scientist, with impeccable credentials as a liberal thinker, discusses "modern society and the rediscovery of the supernatural."

Mere Christianity by C. S. Lewis, Macmillan, New York. Published in 1956, and already a classic. The case for God presented by one of the most brilliant scholars and lucid writers of our century.

Limits of Unbelief by John Knox, Seabury Press, Greenwich, Conn. A passionate affirmation of personal faith by one of the most rigorously honest and open-minded modern theologians.

Process Thought and Christian Faith by Norman Pittenger, Macmillan, New York. A superb introduction to the new school of theology which derives its insights from Alfred North Whitehead, Teilhard de Chardin and Charles Hartshorne. Scholarly yet easy to read.

Guide to the Debate about God by David E. Jenkins, Westminster Press, Philadelphia. A leading British theologian introduces laymen to Bultmann, Barth, Brunner, Bonhoeffer, Tillich and other giants of twentieth-century religious thought.

Twentieth Century Religious Thought by John Macquarrie, Harper & Row, New York. The most comprehensive and reliable treatment of the whole spectrum of contemporary theology. Takes some digging, but if you work your way through it you'll be thoroughly conversant with the issues, trends and problems of religious thought in our time.

God in an Age of Atheism by S. Paul Schilling, Abingdon Press, Nashville, Tenn. A professor at Boston University deals honestly, forthrightly and intelligently with modern objections to theistic belief.

The Question of God by Heinz Zahrnt, Harcourt, Brace & World, New York. A scholarly treatment by one of the most learned European scholars of our time.

The Existence of God, a reader edited by John Hick, Macmillan, New York, A paperback compendium of arguments for and against the existence of God from the time of Plato to the present.

A Christian Natural Theology by John B. Cobb, Jr., Westminster Press, Philadelphia. One of my favorite contemporary theologians demonstrates the compatibility of Christian belief with Whitehead's philosophy and the insight of modern science.

The Living God of Nowhere and Nothing, by Nels F. S. Ferré, Westminster Press, Philadelphia. Particularly useful for those who find it hard to conceive of God.

A Creed for a Christian Skeptic by Mary McDermott Shideler, Eerdmans Publishing Co., Grand Rapids, Mich. A plausible presentation of essential Christian beliefs in contemporary terms, with great psychological insight.

Apology for Wonder by Sam Keen, Harper & Row, New York. A penetrating and witty analysis of modern man's religious hangups.

The Future of Belief by Leslie Dewart, Herder & Herder, New York. One of the most significant theological books of our time, by a famous Canadian Catholic scholar. Hard going for laymen, but rich in fresh thoughts.

The Systematic Theology of Paul Tillich a review and analysis by Alexander J. McKelway, John Knox Press, Richmond, Va. Tillich himself called this "an excellent introduction to my theology." Not easy reading, but vastly easier for the layman than Tillich's own monumental *Systematic Theology*.

BOOKS TO READ WHEN YOU'RE PRIMARILY CONCERNED ABOUT A CONFLICT BETWEEN SCIENCE AND RELIGION

Truths in Tension by John Habgood, Holt, Rinehart & Winston, New York. An unusually lucid book by a scientist who also is a Christian.

The Secularization of Christianity by E. L. Mascall, Holt, Rinehart & Winston, New York. Good throughout, but especially in Chapter 4, which deals with "Science, the Secular and the Supernatural."

Miracles by C. S. Lewis, Macmillan, New York. Lewis restores miracles to a reasonable place as part of God's way with man.

BOOKS THAT WILL HELP YOU UNDERSTAND WHAT THE BIBLE IS AND HOW IT SHOULD BE READ

Your Bible by Louis Cassels, Doubleday, New York. I brazenly tout my own book because it was written precisely to fill this need.

Ring of Truth by J. B. Phillips, Macmillan, New York. The great Bible translator tells why he finds the New Testament convincing.

Invitation to the New Testament by W. D. Davies, Doubleday, New York. Written by one of the world's foremost biblical scholars for laymen.

BOOKS TO READ WHEN YOU WANT TO LEARN MORE ABOUT JESUS.

The Real Jesus by Louis Cassels, Doubleday, New York. Here I go again, touting a book of my own, and my alibi is the same as before: it was written for the express purpose of introducing you to Jesus as he really was, and not as pious legend has depicted him.

The Life and Teaching of Jesus by Edward W. Bauman, Westminster Press, Philadelphia. The well-known television teacher presents the story of Jesus in vivid layman's language and full fidelity to the best modern scholarship.

Jesus Lord and Christ by John Knox, Harper & Row, New York. My own debt to this profound and beautifully written book, by a great scholar who also is a wholly committed Christian, is enormous.

Jesus of Nazareth by Gunther Bornkamm, Harper & Row, New York. One of the most brilliant contemporary German theologians demolishes the notion that we really can't know much about Jesus.

Acquittal by Resurrection by Markus Barth and Verne H. Fletcher, Holt, Rinehart & Winston, New York. Yes, say two eminent contemporary scholars, it really happened.

BOOKS TO READ FOR INSIGHT, STIMULATION AND MEDITATION

Affirmations of God and Man, an anthology edited by Edmund Fuller, Association Press, New York.

The Nature of Man, a reader edited by Erich Fromm and Ramon Xirau, Macmillan, New York.

Letters and Papers from Prison by Dietrich Bonhoeffer, Macmillan, New York.

The Sense of the Presence of God by John Baillie, Scribner's, New York.